Giving Away Your Money

Giving Away Your Money

A Personal Guide to Philanthropy

by

Raquel Newman, Ed.D.

Schreiber Publishing
Rockville, Maryland

Giving Away Your Money
A Personal Guide to Philanthropy
by Raquel Newman

Published by:

Schreiber Publishing
Post Office Box 4193
Rockville, MD 20849 USA
spbooks@aol.com   www.schreibernet.com

First Printing

Library of Congress Cataloging-in-Publication Data

Newman, Raquel.
  Giving away your money : a personal guide to philanthropy / by Raquel Newman.
    p. cm.
  Includes bibliographical references.
  ISBN 1-887563-54-7 (alk. paper)
    1. Charities. 2. Charitable uses, trusts, and foundations. I. Title.

HV40 .N47 2000
361.7'4- -dc21

00-033849

Printed in the United States of America

The act of charity shall be peace

-Isaiah 32:17

Acknowledgment

This Book was made possible by much encouragement, support and valuable suggestions from Lynne Arkin, Allen Calvin, Jeffrey Dekro, Gary Tobin, and Erik Walker. Other indispensable helpers have been Rhonda Abrams, David Heller, Lani Silver. Further support throughout this venture has come from my publisher, Morry Schreiber. A heartfelt thanks to all.

Introduction

This book is written for ordinary folks. Wealthy givers have staff to assist them. People of less wealth may not have staff, but use other resources to assist gift decision-making. Some funders spend a great deal of time and effort on information gathering, assessing and evaluating their charitable giving. This book addresses the dilemma people feel annually, when a stack of requests for funds sits on the desk by December. What to give to? How much to give? How to maintain a balance between areas of giving, and decide funding between one worthy cause and another? How to affect priorities in giving, and what is the proper proportional giving between charitable organizations? This book answers these questions and provides relevant information about giving to give you tools for giving away money.

Why does anyone write a book about giving money away? There are several reasons for writing about this fascinating subject. First, I am personally interested in the subject of philanthropy, its development and practices, as well as the act of making charitable contributions. My interest is based on decades of experience both soliciting funds for organizations and consulting to organizations about fund raising, as well as years of experience of personally giving money away. Second, the independent sector, which is neither governmental nor private, commonly called not-for-profit, occupies a very important place in our social and business structure. These organizations are sometimes referred to as nonprofits (although there are differences) and non-governmental organizations, or NGO's. There are over a million not-for-profit organizations in the U.S. that receive donations. They employ tens of thousands of people with a variety of skills. The third reason I am writing is that like any specialized field, philanthropy requires some understanding and experience. This book attempts to enlarge what you already may know about charitable giving, and have experienced with your own giving. The fourth, and most important, reason for writing about giving away your money is to help you affirm what you value and set the priorities you want to assign to the organizations of your choice. You should have substantial information to use as a template for future giving. You should feel more secure, stronger in your ability to make decisions about giving money away. You will find out what you really care most about and be able to analyze what motivates your gifts. And hopefully, you will feel that the money you are giving away is used effectively, and that your gifts can and do make a difference both to you and to the receiving organization.

In this book I do not recommend giving to specific charities. I have my preferences and favorites, just like you do. I also have both positive and negative attitudes about certain organizations. One can only know a limited number of not-for-profits well enough to make a rational selection. To give readers a so-called approved list would be presumptuous of me. There are literally thousands of fine not-for-profit organizations, covering the spectrum of needs and interests, that function independently. What amount one gives, to whom, and why, are decisions that are intensely personal and idiosyncratic to each individual and family. What I do try here is to give key examples of how to think about the subject of philanthropy, to show what works more effectively in making decisions and what does not.

If, after reading this book about how to go about giving money away, you feel more satisfied, more effective and more confident about the giving choices that you are making, or will make, then this effort has been worthwhile for both of us.

My background includes extensive time served on boards of not-for-profit organizations. As a professional consultant, I have worked with organizations that need assistance with their fundraising and organizational management issues. As a funder myself, I have had the opportunity of honing my skills at asking questions of organizations that I am interested in helping. I have learned to expect information and reasonable answers to assist me in making donation decisions. I have learned to trust people I get to know at not-for-profits. I have also written about organizational issues in the management of not-for-profits. I am familiar with the workings of both family and public foundations, both fast-growing segments of philanthropy. Also, I have lectured on the subjects of raising and giving away money.

Whether you earned all your money, or received an inheritance from family and/or spouse, you choose to give away your own money based on your own motivations and desires. Giving money away is a privilege, an opportunity, a challenge, and a joyful task. It is the generosity of people like yourself that fuels the not-for-profit sector of our society and continues the distinguished tradition of voluntary giving in America.

Chapter I

What's Involved in Giving Away Money

Forms of Giving Vary

E verybody is a giver! Think for a minute about the last time you gave a gift to someone. Perhaps it was a birthday cake for a loved one, or a get well card sent to a colleague, or extra cans of tennis balls for your neighbor and doubles partner. Maybe you have dropped change into a cup for a homeless or disabled person. These acts are gratuitous, in which money and/or goods are given freely from your heart, out of interest, caring and concern for others.

Philanthropy works much the same way. People are givers—they are donors who give gifts of money or goods, and gifts of volunteer time. The society in which we live has endless unmet needs and problems to be solved daily. When we decide to help solve issues and problems with money, donated goods and volunteer service, this act is called philanthropy. In response to requests for help, we perform acts of charitable giving that have considerable value to the receiver of the gifts. Our acts may include placing a one-dollar bill in the church coffer. Our acts may also include multimillion dollar foundation grants that address global issues. Grants may go to promote peace or telecommunications, or towards making education available to children.

Often charitable giving is rewarded with an exchange to the donor. If you buy Girl Scout cookies, the organization receives money and you, the donor, receive cookies. Many organizations reward a gift with a plaque or a certificate of appreciation. They acknowledge their donors with dinners, entertainment, special events, or other kinds of awards. Acknowledging donor support is very important to the culture of charitable giving. Your involvement in the culture of philanthropy can be equal to the value of the money you contribute.

In fact, the American tax system is set up to favor donors. Tax laws allow individuals and corporations to deduct a certain percentage of charitable giving against annual income. These laws let people list their gifts one by one on their annual tax return, or take donations together in a lump sum amount as a standard tax deduction from total annual income. The government thus recognizes the special culture of philanthropic giving. Our government is in partnership with those who are charitable givers. Americans give more money away and give more volunteer time to not-for-profit organizations than any other country in the world. Ours is a generous society. And, our tax system encourages this social behavior.

Tools to Help You Give

You may consider yourself a donor to philanthropy. Whether your gifts total a few hundred dollars annually, or are for much more money does not matter. If you only give money away to some organization now and then, or have made but one or two significant gifts in your life, you are still a donor. Information in this book is meant to help you to consider how you and your family may perform philanthropy in the way that suits you. You will read about how to be more effective and timely in the way you make donation decisions. You will find suggestions concerning the processes to follow in giving your money. Some key issues and their importance to consider will be described. You will be encouraged to consider your feelings associated with giving money away. Do you like to identify and associate with a particular charitable organization? Does it make you anxious to give charity? Do you feel donating is a privilege? Are you acting out of moral obligation to share your money with others? There is no single right answer to these questions. However, you should think about your attitudes toward giving away your money while you are reading on.

You will find important questions to ask those who request your help. You will encounter examples of how others have given their gifts. Included here are actual stories of charitable giving that show you how people have acted upon their strong beliefs and attitudes. With the information available here, you may feel that charitable giving yields an enhanced sense of well-being. You may think of yourself as doing a good job with your available funds. Best of all, with your money you are enabling others to have a better life.

Teaching What You Know and Do

As you make gifts, you learn to be more expert in choosing what interests you, asking questions, and setting priorities for making choices. You can also pass along what you have learned to others. From research completed by professors Paul Schervish and John J. Havens at Boston College, it appears that identification with charities comes from what is labeled "associational dynamics." In other words, *you tend to identify with the charitable organizations with which you are involved.*

What can be more important than leaving a legacy of your personal values? If you have (or are planning to have) children, teach them when they are young to set aside a small part of their allowance for giving away to others. This is the beginning of their understanding of charity. Some families may think that talking about values and money is somehow embarrassing. Actually, both subjects are very much on your and everyone else's minds in the process of living. Your values legacy lasts over time. Money is to be managed—either spent, donated or kept, according to your individual needs and choice.

Values Inform Your Lifestyle

Positive personal values for you and your family inform charitable giving during your lifetime. Clearly, the ability to undertake philan-thropy depends on your individual circumstances. The same ethical principles that govern how you think, work and live with family and friends also inform your philanthropy. Having your donation decisions grounded in values and principles is very important. The ethical grounding to your charitable giving protects you from questionable requests. It keeps you from responding too quickly, without sufficient information or certainty that an organization's claims to your money is consistent with your personal beliefs and values. You should not be swayed by appeals to an activity that is not to your interest or liking. However, we all try to respond to a perceived emergency or crisis.

Giving your money away is formed as a habit. Over time, you get used to making donation decisions. You come to feel comfortable with charitable giving. Correct decisions as well as mistakes teach you what is likely to work, and what does not. Philanthropy becomes part of your ongoing lifestyle.

Always link your personal values with giving money away. As you prepare to do your charitable giving, hold a family meeting. There you can discuss with your family both short and longer range ideas for giving away money. Have younger children give money to some activity or program that they can both relate to and understand. Together with young children, choose one organization, two at most, to assist. Even as young as age seven or eight years, children can learn about sharing what they have with others who have needs. Many families bring their children with them to serve food at soup kitchens for Thanksgiving and other occasions. Many families together help take care of household chores and property fix-up for the elderly. These are ways for children to learn firsthand about your personal values—what is important to you and why. This is an opportunity to develop shared values and common charitable goals together. As the children get older, you can listen to them state their own choices, which reflect their values connected to giving money away. Using this method, you and your children, spouse, partner or friends will grow closer, and can better be held together in the joint pursuit of charitable giving.

In the aftermath of Israel's Six Days War in 1967, people tried to raise money for Israel. As part of this effort, one little girl of seven joined her parents and brothers in a community-wide meeting. In order to help others, she stood up to donate her entire life savings of $3.00. The child had observed her parents' behavior in being involved and generous with both time and funding for their community. To her, helping out was a natural thing to do; she wanted to be counted in the effort.

Talk within your family about the value of money management. Part of that value is charitable giving. You can talk about having impact with philanthropy and how to do so. You can talk about making a difference, both with small and large gifts. Share with your family, good friends and colleagues the philanthropy that you are choosing to do, or have done. Tell people both what the gifts are for, and why you have decided to make certain gifts. You can feel proud of your activities. You can teach others, in turn, by your example. The late Lucile and David Packard, benefactors of the second largest foundation in our country today, gave early lessons in the practice of philanthropy to their four children. When the family gathered around the dinner table, they talked over what was important to them individually and as a family. They discussed how to deal with difficult issues, how to learn about them, seek expertise, and how one might use giving capacity to tackle problems. Thus the family, talking together, found their philanthropic focus.

People follow the example set by others. The reason is that a relative, friend or associate may think that if you consider a not-for-profit's work important, perhaps that person should give serious consideration to supporting it as well. Of course, you may prefer to be private about your own philanthropy, and that is fine. This is a matter of individual preference, and what makes you comfortable. Only the U.S. government requires knowledge of your charitable giving, when you list the amount of money you have given, and itemize gifts, if appropriate to your tax situation.

Author Charles Collier developed a family questionnaire, a useful tool for you to discuss philanthropy with children. Make a list of questions and rank by number what is most important to you and yours. Examples can include career success, financial independence, community standing, spirituality, volunteerism, being creative or giving service to others. By developing your own short questionnaire suitable for your family, you can think about and write up a values approach that underpins all your charitable endeavors.

Chapter II

Values, Helping Others, Rewards

Philanthropy for a Lifetime

Nobody is born an artist or doctor, lawyer, social worker or scientist. People learn about what they want to do, in order to develop expertise and confidence. The same is true for charitable giving. It is an activity that you can pursue over a life time. Do you recall the first time you gave money to someone or for something? Was it to sponsor someone for a walk-a-thon, or buying a raffle ticket for your school? No matter how modest the gift, you probably started giving money away at an early age. Your parent(s) and/or teacher(s) undoubtedly gave you their approval and encouragement when you helped someone else.

How do you become more confident about giving money away? What you do with your money tells a lot about who you are as a person. In philanthropy, your ethical standards, your personal values are brought to bear. Always keep in mind several key points in connection with making a gift:

1. *Core Values.* What do you believe in?

Stewardship of wealth was a major idea, an old biblical reference, that most informed the charitable giving of Andrew Carnegie when he became a noted philanthropist. His ethical basis for giving money away was a belief that he had only temporary control over wealth, in the role of steward. He felt a moral mandate to give money away while he was alive, because he thought wealth is not yours to keep forever. You cannot take your money with you. Carnegie felt that God does not reward a miserly person, disconnected from the world. Just as you have accumulated worldly goods and money, you must give some of those earnings back on behalf of others. Luckily, many philanthropists in America for well over a hundred years have believed that the implicit meaning of giving charity is taking care of those unable to care for themselves.

Another motivator for philanthropy comes through religious convictions. Most Western religions teach that it is a person's obligation to take care of those in need, those troubled, disabled and unable to care for themselves. Part of being an ethical person is sharing what you have with others. These are powerful motivators for giving your money away.

A third approach to philanthropy is based on social justice and the need to repair the fractured world around us. This view means that you are not free from the tasks and challenges at hand. Whether it be through litigation to stop despoiling the earth, or to reform social practices, or help out others, your ethics of social justice may infuse your charitable giving.

Still another values approach is the idea that you live in a community and are attached to it through your work and in your personal life. Being part of a community requires helping it become and stay strong through volunteer time and charitable giving to meet the community's needs. If a community supported you in the past, perhaps you feel a strong motivation to give something back.

Your values may reflect all or some of the above assertions. You may have other reasons for engaging in charitable giving. An exercise to clarify your thinking is to write a one-page statement of all that enters your mind as reasons to give away money. Perhaps it is tax dollars, or your feeling of personal responsibility. Or maybe you received a windfall from the sale of property, or realized appreciation from investments. You may have received an inheritance. Maybe you just won the lottery! What is your burning passion? Are you concerned with over-population, racism, hunger?

2. *Interests*. What concerns and engages you?

Have you a consuming interest in sports? If so, there are scores of charitable endeavors to further sports, by means of training opportunities, competitions, outfitting and sustaining teams, or even assisting the United States Olympic teams.

Are you most concerned with education? Your choices of charitable endeavors are vast. Try to narrow the subject. You may prefer to be involved with small children learning basic literacy and socialization in a class setting. You may wish to further higher education. There is informal and formal education to consider. Informal education may include camping, community centers, programs for after school child and youth groups. Adults of all ages also engage in informal education. Learning can be diverse, international, and broad gauged. Education extends well beyond the classroom.

3. *Outcomes*. What do you want and hope will happen?

Do you want to create opportunity for someone? Do you want a particular activity to take place? Do you want to give back for the good fortune you once received from another source? Are you doing what you think is morally right? Are you doing something that is grounded in your religious and cultural traditions and/or beliefs? Are you someone who genuinely likes helping others in need? Are you trying to set an example for others? All these or other ways of approaching your philanthropy are perfectly valid. What is important is *thinking about* why you are choosing to give money away. Being careful and thoughtful makes the gift unique for you, and perhaps also for your spouse, partner and family as well.

Steps to Helping Others

The medieval philosopher Moses Maimonides listed eight ways of giving, compared to a ladder with eight rungs. Those rungs include situations wherein the receiver knows who gives the gift, or the giver knows who will receive the gift. Or giver and receiver each know about the other. The highest step of giving on his ladder is for neither the receiver nor the giver to be known to each other. For Maimonides, total anonymity represented the highest degree of charity. His model also includes the concept of self-help. The well-known proverb of "Give a man a fishing pole, not a fish," is a way of saying that the best gift is to enable another person to perform on his/her own initiative. And, anonymity preserves the dignity of both donor and recipient.

The next best gift is to enable a person or organization to improve its performance by teaching, or giving money as a tool to do what needs to be accomplished. This is how buildings are built, scholarships are funded, programs are launched. Across America on any day of the year, people are being fed and cared for by others; people are being trained in skill development and educated in schools and colleges. They are being active in sports, church-related activities, and the cultural arts. Your charitable dollar helps to employ many thousands of persons in the not-for-profit field, which represents billions of dollars added to the gross national product annually.

Has the old boot-strap mindset disappeared? Have Americans come to understand and accept that in a post-industrial society not everyone will be able to be a productive citizen? Some segments of the population have no boots, and therefore no straps by which to pull themselves up. Segments of our society have chronic needs based in urban decay, physical disability, broken families, and the traumas suffered of physical and mental abuse. Your charitable dollars work on these issues. At the same time, we have also experienced the enrichment in education, health, the arts and religion or religious-related activities that the charitable dollars you contribute make possible.

Charitable giving has been woven into the texture of life. The notion of giving for designated purposes is accepted. The stigma that the needy are morally undeserving is less powerful today, although people still disdain those who are not like them. It is the middle class and more affluent members of our society who are the direct beneficiaries of much of the increase in charitable giving. For example, it is likely charitable dollars are funding sports, art and theater at your neighborhood public school. It is these dollars that promote health education and publicize access to special health care needs. The charitable dollar is responsible for the growth of theater, dance forms, and art organizations everywhere. It allows new cultural art forms to emerge, and widens access for youth and adults to experience a richer lifestyle.

Rewards of Giving

How is a donor rewarded by giving his or her money away? Gifting means different things to different people. For some, directly helping another person, quietly and without fanfare, is the most significant kind of reward. Others like to be part of a group effort, contributing to a joint fund, involving many people. Still another reward comes with the satisfaction of having considered carefully how to give your money and for what purpose.

When some people are asked to donate money to causes they say that they would like to help out but that they do not have the money to spare. Alternately, they give a very small gift. As long as a donor is acknowledged for a gift, no matter its size, the good feeling comes from being involved in the process of helping out. Another sentiment people express is wanting to be fair to others, and wanting to be a responsible citizen when asked to assist. These are the intangible rewards of giving.

Chapter III

A Short History of Charitable Giving

English Poor Laws Influence Us

The concept of charity is based on religion. Caring for the most needy citizens derives from many biblical injunctions to assist the unfortunate. These concepts are found in both the Old and New Testaments. In 1603, England's Parliament enacted the Elizabethan Poor Laws, placing responsibility for helping others upon local parishes and townships. Almsgiving practices, the giving out of assistance to the poorest people living among them, were part of the church's mission.

Such practices came to the American colonies with the first settlers and continued after the Revolution, as the young nation prospered and grew in size and population. By the early 1800's, local almsgiving was replaced by the development of institutions to deal with a growing set of social issues. There were increasing numbers of orphaned children, or those placed in institutions by indigent parents. Rapid urban growth produced even more sick and disabled citizens, elderly widows, and impoverished vagrants. Some states set up institutions to care for the mentally ill and for children, while workhouses, prisons, homes for widows and disabled soldiers also were in operation. They often relied on community acceptance and support from volunteer crusaders, who pushed public attention toward solving major social concerns. As more immigrants arrived in America and industrialization developed rapidly, cities grew by leaps and bounds. Accordingly, all the social problems increased, causing more family dysfunction and dislocations.

As the frontiers pushed west and industrialization transformed the older settled areas, do-gooders, reformers, and philanthropic patrons worked together to correct the social ills that arose. Antisocial behaviors included public drunkenness, family abandonment, and major crime. People in the cities became frightened. In response, citizens voluntarily went into the public arena to tackle troubling issues. They took their money, experience, and political influence to build major institutions of American life. Our schools, colleges and universities; our hospitals, social welfare and health care services; our religious and cultural arts institutions owe their beginnings to private philanthropy. An example of the development of an institution in the nineteenth century is the story of the beginnings of the American Red Cross. This life-saving organization emerged from the suffering of wounded and sick soldiers during the Civil War. Women tended the soldiers, bringing their domestic skills to help, heal, and administer this organization during the national emergency war years.

In the early twentieth century, social reformers defined the standards and professionalized the fields of social work, health care and the cultural arts. American philanthropy was aimed at making better citizens and making them morally upright. Neighborhood centers and settlement houses, boys and girls service programs, and a number of health organizations that fought disease, unemployment, poverty were founded. Combating the social ills of America's growth society with direct, local services came to be thought of as the correct way to solve social problems.

Social attitudes about philanthropy have shifted dramatically over time. Whereas earlier the relief of poverty was thought to be the church's responsibility, gradually people came to view it as states', and later the federal government's responsibility. Effective political lobbying, and the enactment of much social legislation led to increased philanthropy. Charitable giving was moved from a private matter, performed by individuals, to a public policy serving the community. Passage of the Social Security Act of 1935 capped a series of laws enacted decades earlier, such as wage and hour labor laws and workmen's compensation. With this landmark law, legislators recognized that government had to take more responsibility for the well-being of its citizens.

The role of individual citizens as philanthropists also increased and became more visible. Our tax laws were changed to encourage giving, making charitable gifts a partnership between donor and government. This arrangement benefited both parties; donors received tax relief and the government had its citizens support many organizations and their services that would otherwise be the government's responsibility. The increase in charitable giving contributed to the productive work of not-for-profit organizations.

After the Civil War, industrial growth exploded and as a result, great personal wealth was amassed. Key great givers established the basis for individual modern philanthropy as we know it. The Gilded Age philanthropists generally funded libraries, hospitals, museums, symphonies, and universities with their personal wealth.

Among those best known for placing their individual stamp on giving money away is Andrew Carnegie, whose steel making fortune brought Americans the opportunity of reading books. His gifts included placing libraries in small towns and cities all over the country. Carnegie's philosophy of philanthropy was presented in a stunning book titled *The Gospel of Wealth*. His belief was that he was only a steward, a caretaker of his good fortune, bestowed by the grace of God. He considered performing philanthropy a privilege and, moreover, a duty. To distribute wealth during his lifetime was Carnegie's aim; in fact it became his moral imperative. He supervised the distribution of his money, and at his death all of it was distributed either to charity or other people. His philosophy of philanthropy is still admired today. For many philanthropists, the notion of sharing one's good fortune, of giving back something to society while living, of doing one's duty to help others, is tied strongly to their own religious beliefs.

John D. Rockefeller, considered the father of modern philanthropy, set up a series of foundations with the fortune he amassed from oil refining and distribution. He set new horizons for philanthropy with huge foundation resources. Rockefeller extended the horizons of foundation gifts. His foundation made grants for research, and was the first to focus on addressing worldwide needs. He also founded a well-known school of higher education, the University of Chicago.

Henry Ford, who revolutionized car making with his factory's production line methods, created a foundation that addresses a wide range of subjects, including educational innovation, conflict resolution, as well as technical assistance grants in the United States and abroad. The foundation promotes democratic institution building through planning, communications, and human resource training. The impact of Ford foundation grants, like those of Carnegie's and Rockefeller's foundations, are still felt everywhere in the world.

From these major philanthropists' efforts there grew up several organizational networks for helping members of society. Examples include the United Way, Catholic Charities, The United Jewish Community's federations, and workplace giving with corporate mechanisms to aid and/or match grants of philanthropic donation.

One Gift Can Make a Difference

A relatively small giver, until recently virtually unknown in philanthropic circles, is Eugene Lang. Like the industrial giants just mentioned, Lang grew up a poor child of immigrant parents. He graduated from high school in Brooklyn, became a very successful businessman, and decided twenty years ago to try to give back something meaningful for his good fortune. Lang knew that many disadvantaged youth drop out of school during their teen years. He felt that completing high school is absolutely essential preparation for entering the job market. Lang thought that a desire to stay in school, together with parental encouragement, are key factors for teenagers to reach their potential. He knew that students need to study and work toward a meaningful goal. To give youth incentive to complete their high school education, Lang set up his I Have a Dream Foundation eighteen years ago. It provides a full four years' scholarship for all high school students who graduate from his alma mater and want to go to any New York state college or university of choice. This model of giving has been replicated by other individual philanthropists.

Another example of how one gift can make a difference is seen in the story of Hannah and Charles Logasa's charitable giving. In the early 1960's, research librarian Hannah Logasa and her brother Charles, a painter of modest acclaim, both of them single and aging, wanted to do something to help the fledgling state of Israel become more economically self-sufficient. Hannah Logasa wrote then prime minister David Ben-Gurion that her research showed that the loess soil found in Nebraska, which then produced excellent sorghum and soybean crops without much water use, was similar to soil in Israel's Negev desert. She recommended developing the Negev's vast area's agricultural potential. The Logasas took virtually their total savings and wrote a $10,000 check for the express purpose of growing key cash crops in the Negev desert. The money was used to produce and market sorghum and soybeans successfully, before drip irrigation allowed more diverse farming.

Small Gifts Count Big

Much smaller sums of giving also can make a significant difference when grouped together. Individual gifts of $100 given by many donors to Stanford University's Center for the Lively Arts in Palo Alto, transformed the presentation of the arts in the area. These pooled gifts resulted in renowned performers taking time from scheduled concerts at the university, to go voluntarily into school classrooms, bringing their musical, dance, and theatrical talents to hundreds of school children in the area.

Lang, the Logasas and the many unnamed individual donors to Stanford's Lively Arts organization are ordinary people, with an idea and a single purpose for giving their money away. Their contributions to making our world better have been successful and effective. These donors are not well known, and need not be. Great givers acted on their individual interests by funding huge foundations with their personal wealth with dramatic philanthropic impact. For the rest of us who care about issues that motivate us to charitable giving, there are other ways to be active and important funders.

If you care about the work of a particular organization, it is surprising to learn how your relatively small gift provides added ability for the organization to do its work. One can see this in the story of one giver, named Bruce. In this case, many high school students wanted to attend conferences, but could not afford both travel and conference fees. Bruce supported an organization to facilitate student interest in learning and meeting other young people, but the operating budget had no money for this work. A modest restricted fund was set up within the organization that allowed students to receive a subsidy for specific educational meetings. His assistance helped pay either conference fees or half of the airline ticket. Bruce and the organization agreed to use interviews and a financial need form to screen students eligible for a subsidy. The success of this relatively small gift, renewed periodically when the funds were used up, has enabled dozens of students to pursue their interests in informal education and leadership development. The small student subsidy fund was eventually absorbed into the organization's annual operating budget. A strong idea, backed by Bruce's modest financial support, provided a permanent program for the organization.

Philanthropic history is being made today, not only by the mega-gifts, but also by the small, thoughtful donations made by people like you. It takes commitment and a willingness to undertake a partnership with a not-for-profit organization to further its mission and goals.

Chapter IV

Learning About Giving Money Away

Becoming a Philanthropist

F or some people helping out by giving money to an organization comes easily. It seems natural to help the Salvation Army when a Santa Claus garbed volunteer shakes the little bell on the street during the holiday season. The same desire to want to help leads some to buy a glass of lemonade from children selling at their street-side stand. Others may help to raise funds for new junior league baseball equipment. The impulse to help out makes some people attend school auctions, or contributes towards having them bringing home sweet delicacies from church bake sales.

Mostly, people are preoccupied with making a living, being with family and friends, or relaxing during free time. Nowadays women work too, and there is less time and inclination to pay attention to fund raising requests from a range of organizations. When fewer women were in the work force, a great pool of volunteers was available to the not-for-profit sector. When good fortune advances one's financial situation, earners confront the activity of philanthropy with a different level of attention. The wish or feeling of obligation to help others is sometimes much stronger. We all receive lots of mail solicitation, wanted or not. Phone calls come regularly from organizations, mostly worthy ones, asking for financial support. The requests can be mind boggling, confusing, and even irritating.

Whatever money you intend to give away, you want to give wisely. Do not be put off thinking that because you are not an experienced giver, you are not up to the challenges. Few people are naturally adept at giving money away as they begin to do so. If you want to be a giver, a positive mind-set forms the basis of your activity. You learn from your experiences. Expect to make some mistakes. More important is to learn from your errors, and by remembering them to avoid their repetition. A check list of expectations will help you decide if the organization that receives your gift is doing its part to meet your expectations.

To get your attention and your gift, an organization needs to:

1. Make a case statement for its needs that you can understand.

2. Market its request in a way that captures your interest and attention.

3. Be ready to give you information, answer your questions, and receive you for a site visit.

4. Allow you to take your time to formulate your gift decision (unless there is a crisis at hand), with the help of the organization's information.

If you do decide to give money to a particular organization for the first time, starting with a small gift may be the best way for you and the organization to begin a healthy philanthropic relationship.

Expectations from Your Gift

What should you expect from your gift? What is meant by a satisfactory experience in making a charitable contribution? What does a donor need in order to have a good feeling about a voluntary act of philanthropy? What must the recipient of your gift do with your money?

First, a gift of $50.00 or more should be acknowledged by a verbal thank you, a phone call and/or a letter. When you are asked to continue your support, the repeat request should indicate appreciation for past support. If you are to give a new gift, the organization should let you know that the gift is important and why. You should be informed if the gift will be used for general operating support, or for a specific purpose, such as a building fund, or to match a challenge grant given by another donor. If you ask to see a copy of the budget, the organization should willingly provide one, prior to giving your gift. The organization should be responsive to your questions. Do not hesitate to ask for information to better understand the work of any size organization you are thinking of helping. A site visit is generally quite helpful. Then you can meet the people who run the organization and see their work first hand. Good feelings attained from your charitable giving compensates for the time you put into learning to become a more accomplished donor. *Going through the process to arrive at a smart donation decision is just as important as the amount of money you actually donate.*

Status and Profile of Not-for-profit Organizations

Charity has been institutionalized in America through not-for-profit organizations. Thousands of not-for-profit organizations of all sizes, types, and description are located everywhere. Through the Internal Revenue Service, and each state's equivalent, charities are chartered with set provisions to qualify for 501(c)(3) and/or 509(a) tax status. The 501(c)(3) designation refers to charities that have received both state and Internal Revenue Service approval for tax exempt status, having met certain guidelines. The 509(a) designation determines whether or not an organization is a public charity. An example of a public charity is a community foundation. There one can open an account for an individual philanthropic fund, usually for as little as $5,000. As soon as you gift your own philanthropic fund at a community foundation, you take the tax deduction. You may add to your individual philanthropic fund at any time. You distribute designated gifts by signing a donor-advised form for gift distributions from your fund.

Not all tax-exempt organizations qualify to make your donations tax deductible. Some can only have a percentage of your gift be tax deductible. Ask an organization to send you a letter that states its 501(c)(3) status ("Letter of Determination"). This will clarify for you what you will need to know. With the U.S. and state tax systems, funders are able to make gifts to these organizations while taking a charitable tax deduction from earned income or from accumulated wealth.

Large charities tend to have national headquarters, as well as local or regional offices. They are governed, in part, by a parent or umbrella organization. Their size enables them to seek support from individual and foundation donors. Examples include the American Cancer Society, the Boys and Girls Clubs, Planned Parenthood of America, and Goodwill Industries, organized by chapters and local organizations throughout the country

Not-for-profits are allowed by the government to accept charitable donations. According to Ann Kaplan in *Giving USA* 1997, over the preceding several years fifty percent of all money donated in America went to religion and religious activities and education and related activities. In 1998 it was reported that, for the first time, religion as an area of charitable giving dropped to forty-four percent of total gifts made. The second largest area of giving is still education and education-related activity.

Many larger organizations such as the Sierra Club are technically a lobbying organization sustained by memberships. However, some organizations may have a foundation arm, which has not-for-profit 50l(c)(3) status, as do the Sierra Club and the Nature Conservancy. Both these foundations are dedicated to education and litigation concerning issues of environmental protection and preservation. The legal defense and educational arms within these organizations are permitted charitable status.

The government draws a line between lobbying activities on the one hand and education and legal activities on the other. Lobbying is permitted for legislative purposes, but not for electoral politics. By-laws of not-for-profits usually state that lobbying activities are limited. They may only do lobbying through their national, umbrella organization, or by attaching themselves to a specific lobbying effort.

What to Expect from a Gift

For donors, there should be a direct link between you and the organizations your money supports. Just as there is a link between you and the church, synagogue, or mosque that you and (if you live with another or other members of your) family may attend, or the school your children attend, there is an important connection between you and the organization you are supporting. In all cases, you are entitled to seek accountability for your gift. You should know whether your money goes into a normal operating budget, or if your gift is going for a special purpose. Some national organizations require dues from their local or regional chapter's budget, in exchange for providing central services, such as legal advice, accounting, production and distribution of program and public relations materials. Be sure to ask what the dues policy is, or if the local or regional office splits your gift with its national office. National organizations may conduct their own, separate fundraising effort apart from local chapters, as do local United Way and American Cancer Fund organizations. Many universities conduct general support campaigns, alongside of fundraising efforts by professional schools within their own university, such as law, medical, engineering, or social work schools conducting their own campaigns.

What Size Gift is Right

Organizational size is important to consider when deciding the size of your gift. On the one hand, the American Red Cross appeals to people from all over the United States. On the other hand, it works to alleviate crises from natural or unnatural disasters on the local level. You may wonder if your small annual gift is meaningless, and goes unnoticed to a huge not-for-profit. Consider that if scores of other actual or potential donors were to think the same way, this charity would lose millions of dollars it raises annually. So, even small gifts do make a difference when they are pooled together from many sources.

To consider a different situation, if your child's eighth grade classroom is trying to obtain science study equipment that the school's operational budget does not cover, a small gift may not accomplish the task. Say that there are twenty children in a classroom, and the science equipment will be used by everyone. The teacher is requesting $3,000.00 worth of equipment. Then, your gift needs to be proportionately much larger. There is no national pool of donors to draw from. The donor pool is likely only the twenty parents, or fewer, who consider it important that their child continue science studies with proper equipment. In this case the size of your gift has a great impact on whether the need will be met.

The decision about the size of one's gift is personal and individual for you and your family. Judging the suitability of a person's gift cannot be assessed by a formula because so many factors go into the decision that are particular to the financial situation of the individuals involved.

Give What You Can

A main consideration in giving money is what you can afford to donate. Other key considerations include: what are your personal goals; and what result you desire from your gift? One theory is that charitable giving becomes more meaningful if the gift is difficult for a donor to make from either assets or disposable income. Another theory is that all charitable giving is voluntary in America, and Americans will be generous when they are told of organizational needs. A third theory supposes that as you become accustomed to making philanthropic choices, you find you can actually give more money away than you thought possible. A combination of many factors may go into determining your gift. You need to consider timing. You need to consider your likely disposable income. Who is asking for your support? Is the request for ongoing support, for a new area of your interest, or for a special purpose only? Is the request for a one-time capital campaign? Is it to honor or memorialize someone? These considerations can be both diverse and complex. All requests compete with each other for your donation decision. Experienced professionals concerned with philanthropy know that the psychology of what motivates a donor is often subtle. You may have a combination of family influences from your childhood. Added are your personal ethics and values, and your religiously based impulses. Further, you may have had a particular experience concerning an organization, and the needs it meets, that motivates your desire to assist. A poor experience with a gift will result in your unwillingness to support the organization.

There are some differences, research shows, between how women and men decide to make their gifts. Women tend to give smaller sums and take more risks than men with their charitable choices. Men generally make more money and generally have attained higher levels of education. They tend to prefer giving funds to larger and more prestigious charitable organizations. From survey interviews, one man stated: "little charities are fragile; the big ones [tend to] mismanage." From the same interviews, a woman responded: "Even if [the charity] would fold, I would go ahead and give money." Both women and men respond positively to whomever asks for help, especially in crisis situations.

Many donors would like to help out with more money than they are able to make available. Just as our population is growing, so are the number of not-for-profits and numbers of people making gifts. Having disposable wealth is not an indicator that people can, or will, be generous in performing philanthropy.

Becoming a more effective giver takes some effort and time. Think through your own giving decisions. Talk with others about what level of support for an organization you are considering. Is philanthropy a totally private matter? Realistically, it cannot be. Funders can rarely fully ensure that their own goals are met exclusively through their personal giving. There are always constraints on income, and individual or family circumstances vary. In reality, your donation decisions cannot be measured effectively by anyone other than you and other donors involved. As one donor said honestly, when interviewed: "I tend to favor a cause in which I believe. I respond emotionally, if the cause is right or it is an emergency."

Get Help for Donation Decisions

If your financial situation is complex, do not hesitate to use professional counsel to better arrive at a donation decision. Ask your attorney, accountant, or financial planner for their opinion of the organizational gift you are considering. Ask your advisors how your donation fits in with your other financial plans. Charitable giving and estate planning are directly interrelated matters. Professional fundraising consultants and attorneys can assist you should you consider starting a philanthropic fund or a foundation. Sharing your wishes and thinking is especially important for people who are newly widowed, divorced, ill, or have complex family dynamics. These life cycle events are both traumatic and destabilizing, so it is advisable to seek the opinions of other people. You need to be direct, open, and clear in discussing your philanthropic preferences and concerns. Talking about giving your money away is part of managing relationships with children, parents, and siblings. *It is very important to talk directly with the people in your life who are affected by your charitable giving wishes, plans and decisions.*

Learn by Doing

Donors make mistakes. Giving away money, even in modest sums, will usually result in at least one mistaken judgment about the worth and work of an organization's work. Do not feel guilty or blame yourself for a charitable decision that you consider an error. You made a giving decision based on the best information at hand at that time. For example, a young funder, Sam, expressed his distress over a gift given in good faith to a start-up nonprofit magazine, having a vision to serve readers under age forty. It was planned to have snappy articles on the arts, journalism, culture, politics, and sex. Sounds like it might have a lot of appeal, doesn't it? As a nonprofit organization, rather than a not-for-profit one, this magazine was able to accept advertising. The donors' gifts are still tax deductible. After the second

issue, the publisher went to many potential donors, pleading for
donations because of poor cash flow. He said the advertising revenues
had not yet caught up with the exploding readership. The editor
explained the need to print more copies of the upcoming third issue
of the magazine. The financial request was for interim, or bridge,
funding. This particular donor responded with a sizable gift. What
distressed the donor most was the magazine's turn away from its
intended purposes. The third issue produced was distinctly porno-
graphic. The magazine was repellent to many readers in both its
visual layouts and text. Even the original printer refused to produce
the third issue. In this case, an inexperienced funder was left feeling
that a donation decision he made in good faith was squandered and
abused for purposes very different from what he was led to expect. It
shook the donor's confidence in being able to make a rational
philanthropic choice. Sam needed a lot of reassurance that he had not
done anything deserving of criticism by giving this money. His gift
had simply been misused and abused. Still, he felt foolish, thinking he
used poor judgment, and was a disappointed funder.

When making charitable gifts, you must try to know the people
involved, those who represent a subject and an organization. You
must be able to trust them, in order for you to work well together.

Risk/Reward Ratios

It is risky to fund a new, start-up not-for-profit. You must realize that
a gift to a new organization does not ensure its success. It might not
operate with the integrity that you expected. The magazine just
described used materials that did not break any law, but did hurt other
people indirectly. The magazine editor misused his donors' trust and
exhibited bad taste as well! It harmed the funder by using his gift
money for unintended purposes. The funder learned through this
philanthropic choice that there are failures of organizational integrity
and poor management. Others must have agreed, because the
magazine folded up within the next two months. The magazine gift
experience gave the donor valuable lessons for his future philan-

thropic decision making.

Another case concerns a group of funders' response to their good friend's interesting, innovative plan to set up an independent theater group in Berkeley, California. Here is an example of risk-taking that shows how a start-up philanthropic effort ran into insurmountable problems and folded. The vision of a new theater could not be fulfilled in spite of hard work, enthusiasm, and generous support.

What actually took place? First, potential funders listened to a description of the theater's vision. Having been given firm assurance that people connected with the theater liked the venture, even with lack of a firm statistical data about a likely customer base, the plan was presented to key funders. No one assessed the strengths of other theaters' support, or gauged the competition adequately. Funders were intrigued by the theater's newness, and by strong vision and the special, innovative focus of the theater group. Donors responded with much volunteer time and money. Initial skepticism was overcome by enthusiasm and help. But donors knew little about the subject at hand, and depended upon others with more expertise about the technical, artistic, and financial aspects of running a local theater.

The new theater project limped along unpredictably over two years. A well-known, temperamental artistic director was hired. A difficult landlord provided free space. It was an inadequate site, not centrally located. Publicity was uneven, due to budget constraints. Marketing efforts were too thin to catch much public attention, a common mistake that not-for-profits tend to make. Worse still, the premier production was an obscure play that viewers did not relate to well and were unwilling or hesitant to tell other people to see.

This philanthropic vision flopped for several key reasons. It was an ambitious undertaking to begin with. A start-up theater could not compete successfully with other cultural arts offerings in the Bay Area. The theater did not have nearly the funding it needed to meet costs, and the management was not strong. Many not-for-profits make the error of not raising enough money initially to make a strong foray into business. The founding funder was overly optimistic about the theater's prospects for eventual success. Many funders went along with what seemed to be a shared vision. When the theater collapsed, funders were dismayed at the poor results of their time, work, and money. However, the main funder still kept his friends and no hard feelings persist. Everyone learned that three steps should have been taken. One was to do a feasibility study about what other small modern theater companies there were already in the Bay Area. Had the competition been assessed, the venture might not have been undertaken. Second, insufficient funds were raised to do marketing and absorb the real cost of producing the shows. And third, after initial losses, the theater should have folded up. The risks were there, up front, and all the funders understood from the beginning that innovative theater might not succeed.

If a new philanthropic endeavor takes place, risks have to be taken by funders for a project they endorse heartily. If the theater program had been researched carefully, had good management, lots of volunteers, and strong funding capability, the risks for this new not-for-profit would have been reasonable. Many funders learned a lot from a less than successful giving experience. Learning from mistakes is an important ingredient in giving money away.

Chapter V

Becoming a More Focused Funder

Prioritize Your Gift Planning

P *lanning and prioritizing your charitable contributions is similar to business planning in the workplace.* Like planning for home management, people should plan their charitable giving. The concept may feel a bit strange because it is not usually associated with philanthropic decisions. By making plans for most of your charitable gifts, you actually make the donation decisions easier and more orderly. Of course emergency or one-time special situations come up that may require extra giving that you did not plan for. You can build in a set amount for these needs. The other dollar decisions should be grouped as follows:

1. *Annual, ongoing gifts:* size of gift may vary according to perceived organizational needs, and your ability to give.

2. *Project gift:* which usually is a multiyear commitment, typically to fund a building or designated fund for an organization.

3. *One-time gift:* either for an emergency situation, a special gifting occasion or a building fund.

The planning phase for your charitable donations requires that six key questions be answered:

1. Are you committed to giving from one to five percent of your total income from all sources to philanthropic causes this year? If not, how much in total dollars can you commit?

2. What was the total amount of donations you made the two prior years, and what is the relationship between these amounts and your

incomes? You may be surprised that according to your capacity you gave too little. You may have even exceeded five percent giving because of your own plans and specific charitable interests.

3. Do you expect to give the same amount of money to not-for-profits again? Must you adjust for changes, both for more and less disposable income? People's financial situations vary, unless one lives on a fixed income. Changes in your personal life may affect your ability to contribute as well. Can you handle an emergency request for assistance?

4. What gifts in the past provided the most and the least satisfaction to you? Why? Make a list of gifts made and think about their effect upon you and/or your family.

5. Did your past gifts make a difference to the organization? Is it possible to know this information? Remember the illustration of a teacher needing science equipment for the classroom that only a limited number of parents can help purchase.

6. Did you change your charitable giving patterns? How?

The Business of Philanthropy

Your charitable giving becomes more fun and more satisfying with a plan and a scheme of priorities. Rank your priorities for kinds of gifts, and assign a value to each accordingly. In running a business, one makes a plan for operating, sets priorities, and knows how much the business expects to spend to complete its product or service. In philanthropy, approach your giving in a businesslike way. Set up a schedule, choose your priorities, weigh your interests and funds to distribute, being mindful of organizations' needs. Then decide what money you can give away. Your philanthropic style will be individual to you in making choices. But the methods are similar to being in business.

You are in the business of charitable giving. For some people, this is a task to be faced only at the end of the calendar year. With others, the main consideration is doing the right thing when assistance is required. For still others, the tasks are more challenging and joyful. Others have still another view, for them giving money away is routinely supporting the same activities each year, and giving becomes a rote exercise. For you, the business of giving money away will become more effective as you think about the subject, doing it with planning and assembled knowledge. You will become more confident about both your choices and the sums you give away. You will become a sophisticated funder. Both practice and experience are great teaching tools.

How to Prioritize Your Donations

Prioritizing one's charitable giving is hard because there are so many needs, so many fine organizations doing excellent work and, of course, you have finite means with which to help out. However, think about your priorities by boxing each one separately, and then assigning a value to each boxed priority. This quick exercise will help focus your interests. Earlier, you read about how to decide on the right amount of money to give to an organization, based upon its size, whether local or national, whether new or established, etc. By putting a 1 to 8 ranking in each of the eight boxes shown, you are defining better the strength of your charitable interest, and your preferences for where donations should go. If two or more boxes are of equal interest, use the same rank order number.

annual, on-going gift	benefit, ex-change gift	capital cam-paign gift	emergency gift
special project gift	paying back gift	in honor of or memorial	special inter-est gift

What kind of a philanthropist do you call yourself? Check out the listing below and see which category or categories you fit. You may not want to place yourself in any of the types described. In that case make your own designation.

1. The *"good citizen"* type: includes membership in your child's PTA group, sponsoring a neighbor on a Walk-A-Thon event for a charitable purpose, etc. You are being a responsible and good citizen.

2. The *social graces* type: includes tickets to a benefit performance, attending an auction for the local hospital's auxiliary benefit, going to charity dinner, a school fair. You do these things because you feel you must or would enjoy attending.

3. The *altruistic* type: means that you are willing to do things for others unselfishly. You like to help out. For example, you are not really interested in environmental clean-up, but you know that your community must preserve more open space in charitable trust from zealous over-development. You go to a rally and march. Or, learning that there is a shortage of funds to help recent flood victims in the area, you respond to a special appeal from your local churches for bedding and clothing supplies. You take items from your own household and write a check as well.

4. The *dues payer* type: means your motivation for giving is based on past help received and the need to repay others. Such examples include giving to scholarship funds, camp financial assistance funds, special education assistance, etc.

5. The *religiously based* type: means that your personal belief system is based on religious principles. Giving to religious organizations that reflect these beliefs is of the highest importance.

6. The *tradition* type: means that your parents and grandparents before you were interested in certain forms of charitable giving, and you wish to continue the family tradition. Examples may include your

ongoing support of a college/university, museums, or the performing arts.

7. The *activist* type: means that you identify with organizations that seek social change, through the vehicles of education, lobbying, advocacy, civil liberties, legislation, and political activism. You are willing to be a risk taker, to be on the cutting edge of change with your charitable dollars.

8. The *catch-all* type: means you are drawn to a one-time special situation to support an unusual charitable request. Examples may include a contribution to charity of choice for someone who has passed on. Perhaps it is honoring a major birthday, anniversary or key life-cycle event where the person requests no gifts, but prefers a contribution to charity.

Solicitation Styles Vary

How you are solicited for organizational support may influence your decision to give, and even how much you give. Organizations ask people for help by using the collective "we." They explain the organization's vision and work in "we" terms. But donors tend to personalize their gift giving by saying: "I am giving you . . ." or "because you are asking me, I will give . . ." The task for an organization is to convince the individual that their potential gift is vital, and goes beyond the asking person's request. The person who requests your help is the link between you and the organization that receives your philanthropy. The connection is philanthropy, from which the "I" representing your gift is connected to the "we" of the organization that you make a gift to. For those of you who have been asked many times to contribute, and for those of you who have made requests of others, the importance of a personal connection cannot be underestimated. Personal connections make the organization more personal to the donor. In giving away your money you are not only responding to an organizational need. In the donor's mind, the asker, not the organization, becomes the crucial connecting link to a particular philanthropic cause. It is a person who says "please help," and who then says "thank you very much for your help" that matters. The not-for-profit is the instrument for the exchange, which benefits both you and themselves.

Many Choices for Funders' Interests

American philanthropy has grown to be a big business. It has its own economy as part of the total gross national product of the economy. A few facts about the third, or independent sector, will illustrate its vital importance and growing dependence on participation by the donor population. The number of registered not-for-profits is 654,186 as of the 1998 *Giving USA* yearbook, the last year that figures are available. The independent sector is still growing. The total number of not-for-profits represents 4.4% of all business entities in the U.S. Of total national income annually, the independent sector share is 6.2%, which includes volunteer time.

Below is a breakdown of individual giving to organizations, in billions of dollars for 1997. The source is *Giving USA*, published in 1998. *These are estimated figures.*

Source of Gift	Amount (in billions)	% of Total Given
Religion	74.97	42%
Education	21.54	12%
Health	14.03	7.9%
Human Services	12.66	7.2%
Arts, Culture	10.62	6%
Foundations	11.20	6.3%
Public Society	8.38	4.7%
Environment	4.09	2.3%
International Affairs	1.96	1.1%
Unallocated	15.96	9.9%
Total	175.41	100% (rounded)

According to advance figures for 1998 from *Giving USA,* fund raising rose nearly 9 percent, reflecting the greater values of equities in the stock market and more cash available. As usual, most gifts came from individuals—they represented 85.1 percent of total giving in 1998, including bequests. Environmental group donations rose more than 26 percent, and giving to human services organizations increased by more than 25 percent. Health organizations and hospitals donations grew by 18.6 percent. However, gifts to arts and culture groups declined slightly, at 2.3 percent.

All of the above charitable categories qualify for tax-free gifts to organizations that have achieved 501(c)(3) status. There have been attempts by conservative congressional legislators to pass two bills in Congress that would tax your contributions to not-for-profits. Should such a bill pass Congress, it would remove a major incentive to donors and would harm the ability of not-for-profit organizations to raise money. One bill was to tax an organization for all gifts it received, if the organization does any lobbying. The bill was aimed at such organizations as Planned Parenthood Federation of America, because some legislators disapprove of their family planning work. The second bill was to remove an organization's tax-exempt status if it accepts federal funds for any purpose. This bill would have impacted schools, hospitals, social service organizations, etc. Although the federal government currently helps the independent donor with its tax laws, there are political elements that wish to undermine the effectiveness of many of its organizations.

Deciding on What to Help

Informed charitable decision-making is a process that you can learn by doing your own philanthropy year by year. There is a direct relationship between how much time and effort is spent and the worth of your gift. Obviously, you would spend more time investigating a five hundred dollar gift than investigating a fifty dollar donation. You may repeat smaller gifts annually, without doing much research. However, you will probably want to do a significant amount of research and learn some good reasons before you go ahead with a five hundred or thousand dollar gift.

Chances are that a donation decision at the $5,000 level means that you are more familiar with the asking organization. You know about its operations. It is worthwhile to take time for an on-site visit. This lets you look at the organization first hand and talk with principal staff. If the potential gift is for a new program, be sure that you have seen the written proposal. These materials should state what the purpose of the program is, what need it is filling, what time period the gift is meant to cover, and what is the projected outcome for this organizational effort. A budget should accompany the proposal. Find out if this is a new program, a revision or expansion of an ongoing project. You are unlikely to be the sole funder of a project that requests your support. It is appropriate to ask from whom the rest of the funding is coming. Ask how much of the total cost has already been committed. Ask how the organization intends to sustain the program, after the funding is completed.

Alumni Have Strong Memories

Typically, donors are intensely loyal to the college or university where they received their higher education. Your high school may also inspire deep loyalty. Alumni are a source of major financial support for the school they attended, whether for undergraduate or graduate education. Memories of people, places, and learning at the school you attended provide an important linkage to your school that fund-raisers understand. Schools and colleges keep in touch with alumni, who represent ongoing and future support of the institution. The whole college or university experience is kept alive by the alumni organizations through reunions, special events, graduation, and major graduate anniversary get-togethers. Sports fans like to support popular winning college sports teams. Women, as well as men, follow the wins and losses of their school's teams, regardless of where they live. Other alumni respond more readily to a library campaign. Others pay attention to the development of a department that contained their course of study. Each alumnus may want their school to be the best in a particular way that may not be similar to what other alumni desire for their school. Yet all the alumni are united by their desire that their school be a great school.

People feel loyalty and are often grateful, especially for graduate level education. That study provided a professional degree, their most important credential. The personal return, or exchange, for receiving that education is reflected in your being successful in a chosen field. Years later, many affluent and distinguished alumni are ready to support the institution that provided the opportunity to attain a degree. Professional networking among peers who attended the school also maintains a sense of loyalty. These connections, made professionally or personally, often last a lifetime.

Cultivating Donors Early

Many colleges and universities are no longer waiting for their alumni to be in their forties, fifties, and sixties before soliciting support. Universities in the past have had to wait a long time for a "pay back" by alumni. By waiting, organizations have lost track of their alumni, or alumni have encountered many other concerns in their lives, or have made giving commitments to other not-for-profit organizations. School seems distant from their lives. Schools and colleges are working with students while they are being educated, showing why support is crucial to the institution. Students learn early the importance of ongoing gifts to ensure that institutional needs can be met. By nurturing the students while they are young and present, the aim is to develop loyalty to, and interest in, the education processes. The payoff for an organization comes when graduates become donors early on, bringing steady financial support over an adult lifetime.

The process of cultivating donors is just as important to the donor as it is to the organization requesting support. Donors need to understand why they are being asked, and what the request is about. You need to know what sum you are expected to contribute. Note how well the person asking for money engages your attention. Many organizations are willing to approach donors by a careful, and sometimes, long cultivation process. Philanthropy becomes a relationship between both the requester and receiver. There are unique qualities in that relationship, because donors give their gifts for different reasons, and each responds in his/her own way.

Paying Back, or Paying One's Dues

The notion of "paying back," of giving what was given to you may be a prime motivation for your philanthropy. Paying one's dues with philanthropy is a special hallmark within American culture. Graduates of schools and colleges may view their gift as paying back for help received by means of their education. A donor or donor's family may feel the same need to give back, to show appreciation, by gifting a hospital foundation, or supporting a medical advocacy and education organization that has assisted with their specific health problem. Support of social service organizations is often regarded as paying back for one's own good fortune, knowing that others are not so lucky. For some, charitable giving is seen as the right thing to do as a member of America's society. For others, it is a morally based mandate. Some people have altruistic motives, liking to help other people.

People remember the biblical injunctions to help those in need, to feed the hungry and provide shelter for the homeless, as stated: "open your hand wide to your brother, to your poor and needy in your land" (Deuteronomy 15:11). About giving, it is said "honor the Lord with your wealth with the first fruits of your crops" (Proverbs 3:9-10). These words carry emotional impact. They are well known biblical references about paying attention to those in need.

For thousands of donors, life has treated them fairly and well, whereas others were, and are, less fortunate. People feel a need to do something about the less able, the sick, disabled, or impoverished people in our society. Americans have a long tradition of willingness to assist others with either charitable gifts, volunteer service, or both.

Supporting Less Known Efforts

Popular and well-known not-for-profit organizations that have been operating for decades have built long term donor allegiance. Examples of these organizations include United Way, Boystown, United Negro College Fund, Nature Conservancy, CARE, and OXFAM. Your local institutions are probably well known, such as your art museum, university, symphony, or recreation centers.

It is possible, however, to support less prominent efforts that do excellent work. These may fulfill narrow and necessary missions internationally, nationally, or for only a small area. Some not-for-profits are quite small, have limited budgets, and do not attempt to market themselves very far. Examples include your local hospice organizations, literacy programs, and scholarships for children with academic and leadership potential living in difficult circumstances. Every medium and large-size city, and even smaller communities, have particular projects that require your specific support. Summer work programs for youth, athletic teams, the performing arts, or mounting art shows usually require local citizen support. Some funders choose only to support charities in their locale. Others have diverse interests and try to balance local with national or international charitable contributions.

Research and Development Funding

Other areas of funding concern research and development. Examples include how to manage and cure intractable diseases, or science-based research projects. Organizations undertake feasibility studies which require research about whether to undertake a given project under consideration. Examples of projects which usually require feasibility studies before commencing include a capital campaign for a building or a launch an endowment fund. Frequently, there are evaluation studies for special projects and initiatives that organizations undertake. Another example of how not-for-profits sometimes use research is when they evaluate their own work in order to understand their own success. Evaluations may indicate the need for further research for an organization to undertake.

Donors are less likely to know about the need and worth of helping in areas of research and development. There is no visible product or service to show. What research reveals is information that may be critical for an organization's functions. Organizations tend to seek help from foundations with a history of interest in this kind of grant making. However, these and other less known funding areas can be interesting to you as an individual donor or for your family foundation.

Seeking Affinity Organizations

As a donor, you need to be aware of other organizations whose work reflects your interests, but may not have received your help thus far. Perhaps an organization similar to the one you already support is planning to begin a new program. Perhaps an organization is growing quickly and expanding its presence regionally or nationally. There may be an organization quite similar to the one you already support that seeks your help. The range of environmental protection and conservation groups illustrate this funding arena. For example, a donor involved with support of the Sierra Club Legal Defense Fund, or Earthworks, may learn about Friends of the River, or the Peninsula Open Space Trust, both California-based groups. You may be surprised at the range of projects for which you may have affinity for supporting.

Often mail comes from organizations unknown to donors. One such experience concerns a donor named Diane who receives a lot of mail asking for organizational support. A particular letter caught Diane's attention, because of the organization's attractive logo, or label. The return address was close to her home. The letter's masthead listed persons on the board of directors, one of whom Diane was acquainted with, whom she knew to be a thoughtful funder of good causes. Diane decided to investigate. She called the president of the organization who had sent the mailing. Probably her name for this mailing was taken from a purchased mail list. The organization was considered part of an affinity group, similar to one she already supported.

The potential donor inquired about the organization's purposes. She learned something about its work and most effective programs. As a result of that call, the donor met the principal staff, visited the local office, and was told about a key program that needed assistance. She decided to help fund a person offering technical expertise to new program staff. This kind of donation, supporting a particular person providing technical support, represented a distinct departure from the donor's previous types of charitable giving, one she had not ever thought to explore. Yet the organization's work in promoting responsible, fair mass communication was definitely an affinity area fitting her other charitable interests. Diane's new charitable association has been rewarding, the work of the organization is progressing well, and the donor is satisfied with her new funding strategy. Although her level of funding is small in the scope of the organization's total budget, it is still important for the organization's work.

Chapter VI

Being an Effective Giver

Time is Worth Money

Most people do not spend a lot of time thinking about giving money away. However, philanthropy is a full time pursuit for others. Donors ideally want to feel that the time they invest in checking out charities of interest will be worth the effort in terms of the money given away. There are so many good causes in every city and town in America. There are also many hundreds of charities all over the world that receive funds from American-based organizations. Some examples are religious organizations, educational institutions, and social service organizations that feed and clothe and teach the impoverished here and in second and third world nations. Thousands of national and local organizations do fine work. The March of Dimes national poster child inspired people to contribute millions of dollars for polio research to find a cure. Many of us sold or bought Girl Scout cookies for their annual fund raising drive. Older readers may recall their mothers knitting gloves and scarves for our soldiers serving overseas, or rolling bandages for the American Red Cross and Salvation Army during World War II.

Mail & Telemarketing Requests

Philanthropy, which is defined as the practice of giving away money, is now a much more sophisticated and diverse activity than in the days of bake sales or the famous Shriners circus ticket fundraisers. Telemarketing is a popular fund raising mechanism. Often, we receive less than welcome phone calls at the dinner hour, soliciting funds for organizations we may never have heard of, or about which we know little. The mail may bring requests for money any day of the year. Unwanted print and paper is hard to avoid. You can instruct the post office to suspend all your third-class mail, which includes the solicitations, but mail that is more important may never get to your home. Environmentally conscious people think of "junk" mail, including unwanted requests for charitable support, as wasting precious trees. Charities buy mailing lists from one another. If you wonder how and why you receive certain requests for charitable assistance, most likely your name was on a list sold by an organization you already support. Some mail houses use sophisticated means of selecting your name for fund raising via mail or e-mail.

Fund raising is a year-round effort that raises billions of dollars annually. The asking organization tries to use minutes of your time to obtain your attention and, hopefully, your money. Your waste basket may be stuffed with materials requesting support of charities you do not know or have no interest in assisting. For the most part, charitable organizations have valid purposes. But donors are left confused about which organizations to support, and what issues are more important to address. Charitable mailings can be irritating. To defend yourself, you may respond mostly by ignoring all requests for help. You do not have time to investigate each charitable organization, even those whose purposes and work seem interesting. Moreover, you are not sure how to go about investigating requests for money. How can you be sure that requests are for assistance to responsible organizations? Information-gathering takes time away from other activities that may seem more valuable.

The remainder of this chapter tells you what steps to take to sort out requests for money, create priorities for giving and help you to come to donation decisions.

Maintaining Due Diligence

You can find out about charities in several ways. If the not-for-profit organization has either a local or national address, call the local Foundation Center in your city. Smaller communities will not have this resource, but the local library staff may be able to offer sources of information. If a national organization has an 800 number, it is a good idea to call, ask for a budget, and ask what are the main priorities for the organization's efforts over the next three years. These questions will give you a way to obtain more information upon which to base a giving decision.

Many charities have home pages and websites on the Internet, as does the Chronicle of Philanthropy. This resource provides news and information regarding philanthropic activity, and links to countless organizations seeking support. The Internet is a very useful tool for researching not-for-profits.

Your local United Way organization also may possess valuable information about an organization to which it makes grants. It may know about organizations that are not their grantees that you are interested in. If your city or area has a Community Foundation, it, too, may be a valuable source of information. Ask if the Community Foundation now supports the charity you are investigating, or if it did in the past. If it did in the past but no longer does, ask why there is no continuing support. Use your friends and family's knowledge of specific charities to broaden your own understanding of philanthropic organizations.

Timing is Important

The timing of a request often determines your response. You may be preoccupied with other matters. You may decide to look at the request at a later date. You may prefer to put off even thinking about the charitable requests. You may want to weigh the merits of various requests before making a donation, and set aside time to sort out what you can afford to donate, and what organizations you think are most worthy of your help. As donor, you are entitled to discuss, learn and take time necessary before giving away your money.

If you are considering a major or one-time gift to an organization, investigate by looking at budgets for the last three years and making a site visit, if possible. You are entitled to ask, and keep on asking, until you are satisfied that you understand the goals and operations of the charity. Take the time to speak with those you are close to, people who know you, your interests and concerns. If people in your network are unfamiliar with a specific charity you are considering, they may know someone who is a volunteer and/or supporter of that organization. Find out why they are involved with it and support it. The more you learn and know about a specific charitable organization, the more likely you are to make a strong, well-considered decision about the merits of supporting it.

Reliable information, doing one's "homework," is the best yardstick for measuring if you want to support an organization. By assembling information from various sources, you will have exercised the appropriate diligence before making your donation decision. However, you should keep in mind that there is no substitute for going to the site to meet staff and/or trustees and to see the charitable organization in action. As a potential donor, you may even want make several site visits to obtain a deeper sense of how the organization does its work. This is the time to ask questions to obtain sufficient information for an informed funding choice.

When and How Much to Give

When you do decide to give money, you must choose how much to give. You need to consider the effect of your gift, be it large or small. Your gift may enable the completion of an important project. It may help an organization through a difficult time, or through a crisis situation. There may not be a dramatic reason for your support. You may just want to give general operating support, such as expanding services to a target population, or putting a new roof on a building before winter sets in. Perhaps you are responding to a personal appeal from someone you are close to and respect. Whatever the request is for, be certain it reflects your interests and your beliefs.

In a crisis situation, giving money for emergency food, shelter, or supplies cannot wait. Immediate response in a short timeframe ensures funds for agencies that do relief work.

Is a Major Gift Used Well?

What is meant by the term "major gift?" There is no set rule about what is a "major gift," because each organization sets up its own categories according to its size, program, and budget. The best measure to use in considering a philanthropic contribution in the major gift range is using a baseline of one thousand dollars and above. From the organization's point of view, any donor writing a check for a thousand dollars or more probably has the potential of increased giving capacity. For inexperienced or younger donors, a one thousand dollar gift may seem huge. It is also large for anyone with limited giving capacity. The donor must think through personal giving limits, on both a present and a future basis.

Many a professional school or university can relate stories of alumni supporters who made their first major gift of one thousand dollars, only to increase their level of giving over the years to five and six figures. If you look back at the history of support that you have given to an organization, you might smile about how a gift seemed so large to you years ago. When contrasted with present gift sizes, it was considerably less. However, at the time, you may have had less to give away and may have just begun your association with an organization. Higher dollar amounts of giving partly reflects inflation and the consequent cheapened value of each single dollar.

A young niece, Deborah, used to talk with great passion to her aged Uncle Joe about a charity she was involved with. Uncle Joe made one or two small gifts because of her interest. He knew she gave much volunteer time and donated what little money she could afford. When Uncle Joe passed away, the organization was stunned to learn that he left it a major bequest. He had no heirs, was very devoted to his niece and thus honored her organizational commitment.

If your major gift is used for general operating purposes, then it is harder to know if the gift is used well. Again, the best measure is your understanding and approval of the charitable organization's work. You should be clear about what is to be done with your gift. You should check on an ongoing basis to see how the organization is progressing.

The organization, in turn, should keep you informed with an annual report and program materials that explain how your gift is being used. If your gift is a designated or restricted major gift, or a bequest, the tools for measuring performance are simpler. First, a restricted gift must be used solely for the purposes stated by the donor and agreed to by the not-for-profit. Second, the donor should receive an annual accounting of how much money was used and how. A bequest should state clearly what the gift will be for, spelling out the terms of distribution and how the donor or donor's family is to receive acknowledgment.

My friend Sally recently went through a very uncomfortable process of having to pressure an organization she had long supported, to which she gave a large, restricted gift. The organization was long overdue in giving an accounting of her gift use. Three years earlier, Sally had permitted the organization to "borrow" her restricted gift money to cover an unexpected cash shortfall. She simply forgot about the "loan" of her gift funds, and assumed that the money had been returned to its restricted account. The organization did not ask to extend the "borrow" period. It was very uncomfortable for her to have to remind the organization's executive director that the funds must be returned to their restricted account. Sally insisted that the funds be returned to the restricted line in the budget within a six month period.

A donor has legal basis for an action against any not-for-profit that uses restricted funds to cover its general operating needs. It is important for a donor to work with staff and even boards of an organization. No organization can just ask to "borrow" restricted funds, unless by agreement with the donor, stipulating a limited time period and for what purpose. Even if restricted funds are not being used immediately, they must be held in safekeeping until put to use.

Longer Range Gifts

Other requests, especially long-term physical plans for school, hospital or institution building programs, are called capital campaigns. They are usually designed to provide new services as well. They should be investigated to see how the physical improvements fit in with program services. It is easier to respond to "bricks and mortar" appeals, because one can see from pictures and renderings what a new or remodeled facility will look like. Program plans should be investigated to ascertain that services and programs are not being terminated in favor of spending money for physical improvements.

In all large, multipurpose appeals, the institution does not expect the donor to provide an immediate response. Funders tend to take time to consider large gifts. In fact, an organization must allow time to be able to respond to a potential donor's questions and concerns. The organization must provide useful information as crucial to receiving a gift. Organizations are aware that their solicitation may not result in immediate assistance.

Gifts of Appreciated Property

The IRS has specific rules and restrictions about donated property, such as fine art, rare books, antiques, cars, etc. Any item with a value of $5000 or more has to have a certified appraisal. Both the appraiser and the receiving organization must sign tax form 8283 to acknowledge and certify an items' worth. With most charitable organizations, you are limited to giving no more than half of your adjusted gross income (AGI). When donating property, you are only allowed to use the basis (original value) amount for your donation deduction. If you donate property that has appreciated, you must fill out form 526. If there is substantial capital gain, and you wish to deduct this appreciation, you can only give an item equal to 30% of your adjusted gross income. If the property value is more than the 30% deduction allowed, you may take a "carryover" amount for the next 2-3 years, never exceeding 30% of your income, in order to claim the remainder of the value of the donated property. To claim a capital gain, you must own your property for over a year.

An Unhappy Donor

There are some rather disheartening stories about things that have happened to donors. For example, Yale University received a 20 million dollar gift from a loyal alumnus. He wanted to create a new department, with an endowed professorship and administrative support. Years passed, the university hired a new president, but the gift was never activated. The university's faculty had not been consulted about the gift. Without faculty approval, the president was unable to implement a proposed gift. Eventually the donor lost patience, became disillusioned, then asked for and received his money back.

What went wrong? Probably poor timing or inadequate explanation. The donor was probably not told that the university's president could accept the gift in good faith only after the academic faculty had approved the donor's specific wishes. Not-for-profit organizations must treat all donors with care, respect and interest in their support. Even so, a gift of 20 million dollars is seductive to any organization, even a heavily restricted gift. The university failed to do its part of the job. A gift is a contract between the organization and donor that must fulfill each party's needs and goals.

A Happy Donor

A small gift of five thousand dollars was made by my friend, Tom, to underwrite a charming French language film about the World War II experiences of Algerian Jews living on the fringe of the raging war zone. Each screening of the film at the Jewish Film Festival was sold out, and lively discussions followed with the film maker present. Tom was very pleased by the results of his first effort to support the arts. He felt this film helped make the festival outstanding, and was gratified to have had a role in the endeavor.

Giving as a Creative Effort

Suppose you always wanted to be a dancer, but had no opportunity as a child to take dance lessons or attend performances. No instruction was available, or there was no money for lessons, or no transportation to performances. Perhaps you enjoy theater productions, but you know that ticket prices can be expensive. Many cultural arts productions must be underwritten heavily by the generosity of donors. The actual cost of a performance can be up to twice what viewers pay at the box office, even given a sellout. Many communities offer theater, concerts, dance, and other performances outdoors in public spaces either free or at quite nominal prices. Usually, community-based cultural arts programs are not supported solely by tax dollars, but are further assisted by additional gifts citizens make. Contributing small amounts to a Voluntary Tax Fund, such as the one San Francisco has, provides a variety of cultural performances. Your small gift can go a long way to a communal fund for the performing arts. The donor has the advantage of not having to take time to assess the quality of each event. Many funders' money ensures that programs take place that are available to everyone. Philanthropy that emphasizes the cultural arts have been very popular and necessary, because national funding has been cut back severely in recent years. These gifts are a way of ensuring that artists' creative energies have avenues for free and regular expression in all kinds of public performance.

Your charitable dollars can be given creatively, even with a total of no more than a few hundred dollars to give away annually. Helping a child with special needs attend day or overnight camp, providing help for students' summer arts classes, sports or computer programs can reach a lot of young people. Your small gifts can help make a difference as to whether such activities take place at all.

Government as Your Partner

American tax laws permit not-for-profit organizations to have special standing with the Internal Revenue Service. Recipient organizations can accept financial and in-kind resources from donors. This is not an evenly balanced partnership, because the taxpayer only gets relief up to a certain percentage of the donated dollar, depending on one's tax bracket. The exception is if you have a private foundation or a philanthropic fund in a public foundation, you can receive a full deduction for gifts made. Those that take charitable deductions by itemizing gifts are in a different, and more favorable, category than persons with less income, who give money away in small amounts without itemizing donations.

Freedom of Choice

You have enormous freedom of selection for what charities to support. You give money for special and personal reasons. You have a finite amount of money to give to charitable causes. It is up to you to make informed choices with funds available, knowing that you have thought about your objectives, and investigated charitable organizations you have an interest in assisting.

Often, one responds to requests to give money to an organization when approached by a friend or peer. You are more likely to open your checkbook because of the solicitor's enthusiasm and interest. It is more difficult to say no to someone you like and respect. Nonetheless, you, as donor, are in control. The solicitor must be made to understand that if you decide on a modest gift, or even no gift, there are valid reasons for your decision. Philanthropy is a gift; within that gift reside rational and emotional reasons for your donation.

Start by Being a Prudent Donor

It is a good idea to be prudent about donating money to charity. You may be unwilling to take much initial risk in supporting an organization new to your interests. Perhaps you must weigh cutting previous gifts for another organization, in order to help the new one that now has your attention. You can always increase an initial gift. Organizations understand that their job is to not only obtain your gift, but sustain it and your interest. If they do well, report their accomplishments and ask donors for ongoing support, most likely you will be eager to respond. Your initial gift always contains an implied promise of "more" the next time you are asked to help. Steady gifts from donors are the lifeblood of all charities.

Ongoing, regular donations fuel the not-for-profit sector of the American economy. However, the same size gift given to an organization over a period of time does not take inflation into account. Therefore, the worth of your gift declines in real terms. When an organization points this fact out to long-time donors, they may take offense. The donor may not think of a gift as tied to the cost of living and reality of the marketplace. If a thousand dollar gift given for a long time has declined in real terms, so have all your other long term gifts. Donors tend to think in terms of their gift size alone, and often fail to adjust their thinking about the over-all present worth of their philanthropy.

Is it better to give larger amounts to fewer not-for-profit organizations? Some donors think help goes farther by giving a little bit of money to a large number of organizations. It depends on the nature of the organization, the timing of your gift, what your giving objectives are, and of course, how much you have to give away. In all cases, your philanthropic effort is valuable, even when you are unable to note direct results of your generosity. Not every donation makes a difference to the receiving organization. However, even a gift of a few hundred dollars can be very important if placed strategically.

Creative Giving Requires Objectives

What are your objectives for your charitable gifts? You may be drawn to helping a small, struggling organization survive. You may want to set up a scholarship, camper financial assistance fund, or fellowship. You may wish to involve family and friends in a project dear to your heart, such as a special education need, or health service. Maybe you are interested in research, and want to ensure that a program is reported on, or an evaluation of an existing program is conducted. You may want to do a needs assessment about whether a particular service or capital facility is needed, and should continue. Perhaps you are interested in affecting social change.

It is best to work with the organizations that have the most expertise in your subject area of concern. Given the immense diversity of philanthropy, there is likely to be a not-for-profit doing work in your area of interest. You have to find it. By your own investigation, you will not have difficulty in connecting with an organization doing work in your subject area of interest. Your own investigation helps build confidence about the decision to give.

Organizations often seek fresh notions, so that your creative thinking may be well received when presented. Perhaps the organization is doing already the kind of project or program you have in mind. You may be persuaded to support the effort now in place. If your ideas are turned down, do not be discouraged. It only means you have not yet found the appropriate working partner in your search for creative philanthropy.

Feeling Good About Writing a Check

Giving money away is a joyful task. People may see it as both difficult and easy at the same time. To pay small annual dues to the PTA or to a local "friends of" organization is relatively easy. To consider making a major charitable gift for the 25th class reunion of your high school, college, or graduate school is much harder. In these cases one may feel pleased and successful. In the first example, you are giving as part of a bigger group project. You are not deeply invested with many emotional and rational reasons concerning the donation decision to the PTA organization. In the instance of alumni giving to mark a major class reunion, one is flooded with memories of people and experiences in connection with an institution. These complex associations may require more time and thoughtfulness to make a donation.

Why is there sometimes stress associated with making a donation decision? Why does a life cycle event like the class reunion present a harder decision? Because in this instance you will want to think about your gift, considering the special reunion event that is taking place. Think of the merits of your gift, what it may mean to the institution you know and were, or are, involved with. You wonder if other class members are going to contribute. You should reflect on what your gift may mean to you and your family. Give yourself time to weigh not only how much you can give, but what you want your philanthropy to accomplish. Will it be noticed if you donate, say, a hundred dollars? Is it for a particular class project, or for general support of the school? How much can you "stretch" to make a bigger gift for this special occasion? How do you translate good feelings about your school into a charitable gift? What other interests and organizations are competing for your charitable giving dollars?

At least half the fun is thinking about the processes of giving. The other part of charitable giving is knowing how to make your gift wisely, with confidence, and leave you, as donor, feeling good about giving money. Feeling satisfied about your donation decision is your reward to yourself.

Let us look at a few methods for making your gift:

1. Gift Giving goals: have a budget for donations, look at giving in terms of impact on taxes; plan other gifts of lesser size during the years you may be paying out a pledge for a specific giving project.

2. One-time gift: one check to an organization for the special event, such as honoring an individual associated with an organization or school, or celebrating a major anniversary of an organization's work. Advantage: to be acknowledged as part of a group project, and participate in the event, to feel satisfied with your gift of money and presence.

3. Multiyear gift: the size of your check to be split over two or more years. Advantage: this kind of donation times and distributes charitable giving to accommodate your finances, and requires you to make a giving plan for your philanthropy.

4. Challenge gift: your check is conditional upon other moneys being raised by the organization first. There are many terms that may be set out to define the terms of challenge grants. They include time limits to raise other funds, who will do the fundraising, publicity about the challenge, etc.

5. Matching gift: your check is set up on a match basis by others. This type of gift is more commonly used by corporations and family foundations, to stimulate wider community response. It may be used by individuals as well. Matches may be set as one dollar raised to one given, or higher. For example, the corporation you work for may provide a means to match each dollar you give. Therefore, your gift is effectively doubled. Another example is for every three dollars you may give, a match of one dollar is made by another donor source. Your modest gift is challenged by this technique, and is leveraged by another donor source.

People use self-interest and rational choice when making their charitable contributions. For example, in many instances donors compare themselves to others when giving. They compromise their wishes in order to achieve certain goals. They may change their priorities in giving, in order to address problems. Their wishes influence how and where a gift is made. Sometimes in-kind or restricted gifts are sought by the donor. A limited number of donors desire to give anonymously. If the gift is large, a donor may wish to include a matching or challenge grant to their offer of philanthropy.

You have the freedom to decide who to give to and what to give. Plan what you want to accomplish with your gift. Think about the effect of your gift and why you are making it. Philanthropy is a habit worthy of planning, and one which becomes more interesting, more satisfying, and more successful as you repeat the process. With experience you become more adept in managing requests for help. You gain confidence with each philanthropic decision.

You should understand the steps you plan to take in making each donation decision. The not-for-profit sector is growing as a measure of the economy, and your participation is part of this significant growth.

Chapter VII

How to Face the Future

Responding to Crisis

W hen the Loma Prieta earthquake hit the San Francisco area in 1989, people rushed to respond. People helped out in a myriad of ways. Families of those dead or injured were comforted. Hospitals, fire fighting squads, police, and ordinary citizens pitched in to help out. Neighbors provided candles, flashlights, and foodstuffs. Strangers spoke to one another, people drew close together over nature's frightful happening, which fortunately caused less damage than the 1906 San Francisco quake.

Crises invariably motivate donors, as their emotions are aroused. However, organizations usually do not experience dramatic crisis situations. Most not-for-profits are not in business to meet emergencies, per se. The American Red Cross and the International Refugee Committee are exceptional in so far as they are always ready to operate in times of disaster. CARE or OXFAM send survival food packages regularly to citizens in countries around the world. A real crisis, such as mass hunger in third world countries, or the floods in Nicaragua and Honduras requires rapid response for people left homeless, injured and hungry.

Helping Quickly Counts a Lot

Crises responses sometimes may impel you to make exceptions to regular giving practices. Americans are known to be generous of spirit, and willing to help out when others are in trouble for reasons beyond their control, such as a natural disaster or a dreadful accident. Responding to crisis with your check really does help in providing short term relief. One reason people respond readily to requests for emergency care is because a donor has probably experienced some kind of crisis, and may know about receiving care from another person. A prompt response in the form of cash or checks matters a lot. It is easy to picture yourself in the similarly difficult situation. Doing a special favor for strangers in need feels appropriate. Americans generally want to do the right thing. In some instances, donations of food and clothing are suggested. Goodwill Industries and the Salvation Army are specifically set up for these kinds of gifts. Making occasional donations of this kind are understood as being legitimate, timely, and praiseworthy.

Cash Flow Problems

Steady cash flow can be a problem for not-for-profit organizations. It puts a strain on their ongoing operations. A good example of this problem is how food banks have to strain to maintain daily feeding programs, year-round, despite the fact that donations peak during the cold holiday season in December and January. People tend to forget about supporting food banks in July. Similarly, schools and universities may not be in full session during the summer, but ongoing costs continue. In fact, costs are highest in summer when repairs are made and new books and supplies are ordered. Low cash flow at certain times of the year, summer especially, is a problem for many organizations. If you can make your gift at a time other than the end of the year, when donations peak, it is helpful to the receiving organization. Even splitting your gift into semi-annual payments, or making serial or monthly payments, helps assure an organization more steady cash flow.

Crisis Unleashes Dollars

Organizations use crisis response as a fundraising tool to evoke donor emotions. It is important to recognize that when some organizations speak of crises they may be portraying them in a less than truthful manner in order to promote themselves. Portraying crisis is a proven successful marketing tool. For example, a well-known national organization, known for its defense against ethnic and religious defamation, uses mail appeals year round to announce an ever-growing threat of religious discrimination, even when survey data shows otherwise. Getting donors' attention by playing up their natural anxieties does pump up donations. Some not-for-profit organizations use the fear of antisocial, racist and negative group stereotyping to obtain more charitable giving. It is up to you to be aware that some organizations promote fear and anxiety to seek funds. Such fund raising techniques are probably questionable, but they are not illegal. All the same, it is not acceptable organizational practice.

Do investigate assertions made by an organization asking for your support. A number of years ago, Boystown regularly sent out, twice yearly, a fund raising appeal. They asked for donations in providing foster care and education for their boys in this renowned residential setting. The public did not know that Boystown's residents had declined from about 2,000 to less than 500 boys, with reduced staff and reduced operations costs accordingly. However, annual fund raising revenue continued to climb, as Boystown's population decreased. Investigative reporting by a local weekly paper, The Omaha Sun, revealed in detail the problem situation at Boystown. The story gained the newspaper a Pulitzer prize for investigative reporting. Boystown's image was sullied. The organization was compelled to look seriously at itself, and subsequently alter many aspects of its operations. Boystown fund raisers had to restore the credibility their donor base had come to rely upon.

Planning, Fundraising, and Gifting

Some not-for-profit organizations keep doing the same things, in the same way for years on end. They change very slowly and meet change with reluctance. People remain loyal and rely on longtime association in making their gifts. They approve of the organization's mission to give their support. If you have given to an organization for a long time, but are not quite comfortable with the work going on, stop and ask questions before continuing to give your money.

It is fine to ask an organization what their goals are for the year, or the next three years. Ask to see a mission statement, which sometimes is called a shared vision statement. The statement is like a very short business plan for enterprises. It says what the organization is and what it wants to be. It is equally fine to ask how much new money is being raised, and what priorities have been chosen and why.

It is also okay to skip your support for a year or two, and wait to see how your concerns are addressed, or what changes are being made. For example, if a direct service agency for teens is failing to respond to their needs, and you have a major interest in helping teenagers, find out what is going on before giving your support. Planned Parenthood of America has periodically come under fire by those who do not wish teenagers to receive family planning information. If you are uncomfortable with such pressure, and think that teens ought to be informed and prepared to act in a responsible way as they mature, you need to overlook the negative politics of family planning, and continue to lend your support. On the other hand, if you are against this organization's policies, you will not give it support.

Special Focus Giving

Many donors have a narrow focus for their charitable giving. If donors have children's health as the focus, then these donors may choose not to contribute to organizations working on child legal advocacy and children's learning projects. But children's legal status, education, and health are all interrelated. It may be wise to expand your focus from strictly health issues. You may wish to expand your interests to child enrichment programs, children's disabilities, or social welfare needs.

Sometimes donors shift their focus after giving support to the same organization for a number of years. Some donors target their gifts to local organizations only. The reason is often that they feel they can know about, read about, or visit the organization; it is reachable and feels close at hand.

Size Does Not Determine All

Large national organizations are appealing to many donors because they are known, seemingly safe places to put charitable dollars. Large organizations have certain economies of scale, such as the ability to market, send out mass mailings, do telephone solicitations, etc. These advantages make it easier for large not-for-profits to capture your attention and donations. The downside of supporting only national organizations is that sheer size eliminates knowing the operations thoroughly. Furthermore, size does not always equal effectiveness or efficiency.

Indeed, many donors prefer a small, more local organization because they feel with small organizations they are more likely to know its work. Smaller organizations sometimes operate more effectively. Many donors prefer a more personal connection with a not-for-profit organization. Research shows that women especially prefer to become more knowledgeable about an organization's work, staff, and mission. Men are generally more concerned with the issue of efficiency. From survey interviews, one man said: "I like to follow where the money goes; what it is doing." Another woman interviewed said: "I need to have a connection to an organization. Otherwise it can be run inefficiently, and [I] would not know it."

People tend to support the last place they went to school. Those who attended graduate programs tend not to support their undergraduate school, college, or university. People often like to support large and prestigious institutions, because they are already well regarded. In fact, most smaller institutions have a greater need for money. A gift you give to a small school goes further in dollar value, and may be received gratefully. The same size gift given to a large institution that receives high levels of support may not be as meaningful to the school's operation.

Newer Kinds of Giving

Donors have several options in choosing newer funding strategies. One is to help fund research. Another is a planning grant, which assesses whether a program under consideration is cost-effective for the organization you are interested in. As the work unfolds, or after it is complete, program evaluation is a key tool to measure a program's effectiveness. A funder ought to consider that these kinds of philanthropic grants are as worthwhile as giving money away for either direct services or capital fund drives. The traditional means of helping are for direct services, such as scholarships or support of institutions providing direct social services. You may be willing to help with needs assessment, planning, evaluations, or research in making your charitable donation decisions. These are more subtle, less outwardly exciting, aspects of organizational needs that are still very important in conducting the business of philanthropy.

Examples of alternative program giving include helping to fund an assessment of whether a capital campaign is going to work out for an organization. It might involve support of research on vexing subjects, such as investigations of how the AIDS disease works, or research on how medical, social, and psychological interventions can assist HIV sufferers. Money may be needed to help evaluate how well a program is going, say, in delivering day care for the well elderly. There is a risk attached to this kind of donation that the research or evaluation may show that the organization's efforts are not successful or will not be successful. A needs assessment, preliminary to a capital funds drive, may show that a new building is not possible to build based on projected donations for the project. A program may have to be abandoned after its evaluation, because it is serving too few people for the costs involved. This sort of result may be frustrating to those who have supported the research. However, in these circumstances the funders should keep in mind that they have saved the organization from making a costly monetary, time, scientific, and/or policy mistake(s), or, in some cases, have prevented these mistakes from continuing.

The Role of Advocacy

The funding of advocacy work is a special form of charitable giving. Two examples of advocacy organizations are the Friends of the River and the Mono Lake Committee, both in California, which oppose the diversion of water for uses that disturb the environment. Both work on this issue through legal advocacy. Some advocacy roles center around lobbying efforts or helping to draft legislation that affects a particular population. For example, The National Center for Youth Law drafts legislation and litigates protective services assistance on behalf of youth and for juvenile facilities. This organization improves laws for juveniles and makes certain that juveniles are protected by the laws. They also lobby legislators on behalf of their programs.

Advocacy donations include giving money for planning, assessment, or evaluations. It is one sophisticated way to give money away. This way appeals to funders who know that there is already a large base of donors who will continue to give their funds in traditional ways. These forms of giving open up new ways for you to use your charitable dollar.

Remember how the March of Dimes drive produced millions of dollars annually, with the poster of the polio-crippled child displayed everywhere? This fund raising technique continued even after polio was virtually eradicated in America with an effective vaccine. As revenue declined further, it became clear that the organization had to reinvent itself. An emphasis on polio was replaced by a new emphasis on research to cure severe birth defects. This new emphasis has been effective in attracting supporters, but not to the extent that polio did. There was once a genuine crisis, as people were very frightened about the dread paralytic disease and wanted to respond generously with their money.

How to Pitch in to Help Out

How do you sort out a real crisis from a merely advertised one? It is a good idea to stop and ask questions before making a donation. To have your questions answered, feel free to call, fax, e-mail, or write the organization making its appeal. Ask for documentation about their work. Find out how your gift is to be used. State your concerns openly, and then, if you are convinced that a crisis is being portrayed genuinely, you may respond quickly. You have to have confidence that your charitable dollars will be used for a genuine crisis, and not a fake one.

Beware of organizations that do not answer your questions well, or are fuzzy in explaining the work they do. Often the person soliciting you is versed in only a limited way about the operations of the not-for-profit. In that case you may need to speak with someone in program work. Helping an organization that does not do its work effectively can be compared to buying a product that does not turn out to be and do what is advertised about it. As the client, you should be attuned to marketing techniques designed to arouse your emotional response. A great deal of money is spent by organizations for promotional materials that talk about organizations' work. It is up to you to gauge the truth behind the organizations' advertising.

Does the description of the crisis seem realistic? Is it as bad as it appears from the pictures and printed materials, the news, the solicitation? If the solicitation is by phone, you may be caught off guard. Listen to the appeal, tell the caller you need to think about your response. Request support materials, especially if the organization's name is not familiar. Again, if you are familiar with websites for charities dealing with crises, you can compare what other organizations are doing. Then go with your own best judgment based on the information available.

Waiting to See What Happens

A one-time gift connected to a crisis may be concerned with reconstruction of buildings, programmatic materials, and supplies. It may mean basic help for people in terms of food, clothing, and shelter.

With the cutbacks in federal funds for public schools in recent years, some state school budgets have been pared so severely that teachers may lack basic materials of paper, pencils, and curriculum items. Appeals to students' parents for help may be hard for families who are on tight budgets to respond to. Some parents think that their tax dollars ought to cover all school needs, so that providing class-

room materials is not their responsibility. Older parents in an impoverished school district say they paid their dues when their children were
in school and now it is someone else's turn. These parents make a valid
argument. Even so, teachers may not be able to teach properly without
the proper tools. One short term response is to try to get parents'
contributions. Parents' individual contributions need not be large
providing that many parents respond to the schools' budget crisis. The
longer range response is to tackle the politics of school funding and
seek relief, which is usually not an easy task.

Conditions Made Worse by Disaster

In society shelter, food, and clothing shortages are either chronic or
result from a disaster. Fortunately, many donors maintain the Salvation
Army, The American Red Cross, local Y's, and a huge number of
church, synagogue, mosque, or federated organizations related to
offering family and children's services. Most of these groups are
equipped to help with emergencies quickly on both a physical and
psychological level. They perform direct social services. In both these
situations delay may be very costly to those in need. There is no luxury
to wait and see how things will turn out. The need for immediate
assistance is clear and present.

However, there are certain needs after a disaster which are best
dealt with through a slow and considered response. For example, this
approach is appropriate in the aftermath of earthquakes when dealing
with the reconstruction and retrofitting of buildings. The Federal
Emergency Management Agency (FEMA) provides assistance with
government dollars for a great deal of restoration work. Frequently the
money does not arrive quickly enough to cover substantial costs for
either relocation or repair work that local and federal governmental
units require to make buildings safer. Repair for interior damage to
large buildings requires expensive construction work, sometimes
including retrofitting. A number of churches and synagogues in San
Francisco still need to raise funds for retrofitting. In addition to money
coming from government, congregants are asked to help out with both

money and volunteer work. Older churches and synagogues often lack American Disabilities Act approved ramps and bathroom access. Physical damage may require replacing carpeting and furnishings. Damage from a natural disaster provides the opportunity to address repairs more comprehensively. In the aftermath of crises that lead to building damage the appropriate response is frequently a multiyear payout on a gift for the capital fund drive.

In cases of building reconstruction after a crisis, it is a good idea for a potential donor to wait a while before donating. You should ask to see clear plans for renovation and rebuilding. You should be thoroughly informed as to costs, procedures, and timetable for doing the work. You should see graphic representations of how the building(s) will change and appear after repair. You should ask from what sources the money is coming and how many years you can take to pay out your building pledge. You will make the most intelligent decision if you have the most information available about both physical and program plans for the future.

Do you consider this project to have highest priority in your giving? Are you willing to pledge a multiyear gift? Will you consider participating in an endowment fund for the purpose of both retrofitting your organization's building, and ensuring its long term upkeep? To enhance your donor skills, ask questions about the construction project, and be satisfied with the answers before you commit funds.

A One-Time Gift

What defines a one-time gift to a charitable organization? It may be a long-planned donation that you determine to give to your religious organization or college in celebration of a major moment in its organizational history. It may also be to celebrate a dear friend's birthday or wedding anniversary. Perhaps someone special to you is being honored for good work done on behalf of an organization, and a large gala event is taking place. In all these cases, you may want to recognize such achievements by your gift and presence. Usually, you would not place these donations on your preferred list.

For a less than happy reason, you may choose to honor the memory of a close friend or relative with a donation to an organization, or activity, with which the person was deeply involved. One such story is about the sudden demise of an energetic man in his early eighties, felled by a massive heart attack on the tennis court, one of his favorite sports activities. Two longtime family friends decided that the deceased man should be remembered by what he loved doing. They wanted to honor him and his interests, and give his loving wife some acknowledgment of his life pursuits. So, they contacted the Israel Children's Centers Association, a not-for-profit organization that admits kids at age eight until age sixteen to learn tennis at centers scattered around the country. In addition to teaching the game of tennis, the eleven centers teach sportsmanship and interpersonal and social relations. All centers are open to girls and boys of all faiths, regardless of who can pay the fees. A most improved player award for a child at each of the centers was established in the friend's name. The cost was not high. The man's family was delighted. They felt that their beloved husband and father would have liked nothing better than his name attached to tennis for children's development. He himself had mentored many young people in their pursuits of sports, education, and career goals. Charitable giving was a way of tempering deep personal loss of a friend in a way meaningful to both donor and recipients

Responding to the Solicitor

Suppose that your town or neighborhood badly needs to improve the park where kids play ball, dogs are walked, and you pass the area by car or on foot every day. Suppose a bond issue failed, whereby the voters did not want to spend tax funds to improve the park. Your children are grown, you no longer have a dog, and you do not enjoy the outdoors especially. So, you voted against the park bond issue.

However, your workplace colleague is part of an ad hoc committee formed to fund the renovation of the park. Your colleague phones and approaches you in a self-righteous way, lecturing about the merits of renewing and refurbishing the park, and how it is your responsibility as citizen and neighbor to make a sizable donation. You do not mind being asked to help, but you do feel offended by his pressure and style of asking. You turn away from his appeal and say no. Your colleague shows his displeasure at your response.

The following week, a quiet-spoken neighbor, whose kids went to high school with yours, who attends your church and occasionally goes fishing with you, calls and asks to visit with you. You go off for a cup of coffee. He talks about his good feelings in taking part in the park renovation project. He explains he is a volunteer helping raise the needed money that will give so much pleasure to many families of all ages. He explains how beautiful the park will look when fixed up. He reminds you of how often you talked about growing up on a farm with lots of grass and room to play. He does not ask you directly for a gift. He talks about what the park project means to him, and why he is committed to help it be a success for the community. Finally, he says he would like for you to join in the effort. He tells you how much money he is giving and asks if you can make the same donation.

Your neighbor made the case well for renewing the neighborhood park. He told how he felt about the project, why it is important to him, and what it will do for others. He is open about hoping you will join in the project. He does not pressure you or make you feel guilty if you do not give a gift. He encourages your support. You then feel good about being asked to help out. He lets you know your gift is valued. It is your choice to decide about making a donation. How you are asked to make a donation, and who asks you to give money makes a great deal of difference.

Asking for Money with Sensitivity

The most successful and established not-for-profits know that how they present their needs, and who makes the presentation, matters a great deal. However, there are many small philanthropic projects, such as the fictional park project described above, that also need to raise money. Small and medium-size organizations must treat potential donors the same way as big organizations do, in order to get and hold the donor's attention for a gift commitment. Donors have the right to be treated with sensitivity and respect, be listened to, and be presented honestly with facts. They should be made to feel good about supporting a project. Donors should not be made to feel badly for saying no. The proverb "ask and ye shall receive" only applies if the asker does the job effectively, and the solicitation fits the individual circumstances and interests of a potential donor. Donor cultivation and ongoing expressed appreciation to donors are hallmarks of fundraising success.

Chapter VIII

Chase Your Own Dreams

Helping Others for Special Reasons

An old friend, Susie, confided that had it not been for the personal attention that her high school principal gave to her, immediately following her father's untimely death, she would not have been able to continue to attend classes at her prestigious private high school. Her principal's steady interest, warmth, and support helped her out of her depression. The principal encouraged Susie to do well in academic and extracurricular activities. He insisted that she apply to top colleges, some of which ultimately admitted her. My friend Susie never forgot those dark months as a teenager when it seemed her world had fallen apart. Unable to speak about her feelings of grief and loss with her mother, who was depressed and distraught over the loss of her husband, the wise and kindly principal helped out.

Only much later did Susie learn that the mother of one of her school mates had provided scholarships for situations of sudden need such as hers. Help came to pay the school tuition, which Susie's mother could not afford after the death of her husband.

Both my friend and her brother finished high school on scholarship. Both went on to college and received graduate degrees. Both have made their mark in the world with very successful careers. However, they never forgot the opportunity given to them. Their joint dream was someday to be able to pay back for their own good fortune. Together, the siblings set up a scholarship fund at their beloved high school, so that they could provide financial help for children who had special need to receive support. They saw the need to help replenish the wellspring that provided critical financial sustenance to them and their mother at a bad time.

A Lesson Learned

Susie learned that helping another person in a personally relevant way can be very fulfilling. Many decades later, Susie and her brother were able to fulfill their own long-held dreams of being able to provide their high school with scholarship funds. They were intent upon paying back both for past help received, and also for their own good fortune. Now others are able to experience the high quality education they had enjoyed. It was this scholarship assistance that allowed the siblings to graduate, go on to higher education, and pursue successful careers.

Often donors undergo a life-changing experience with illness, or the death of a dear one. Such an experience creates an awareness and determination to somehow give back for the help and attention they received. People may wish to give volunteer time or donate funds in a specific health area that affected their family. As people undergo the drama of serious illness, its diagnosis, treatment, healing, or death, the value of care received is considered seriously. Health and well-being become of prime interest. People respond with donations to a medical center, a clinic, or a foundation that deals in education and human care. Many not-for-profits are concerned with health and well-being. It becomes very important if your life, or the life of a dear one, is restored to normal. The pay back is literal, and provides psychological support for you and your family.

Priceless Volunteers

Who has volunteered time on your behalf over the years? Who are the people who cared enough to advise, teach, and show you a pathway? Can you think of someone who may have enabled you to advance in your life? A teacher in school? Someone in an after-school activity? Was it your parents, older siblings, or caring relative? Who fostered your specific dreams and interests? Who expressed confidence and concern about your welfare? These people fostered your specific dreams and interests, all on a voluntary basis. They gave time and knowledge generously.

The entire not-for-profit sector depends heavily on continued volunteer time given. Its worth is priceless, in terms of measuring hours, effort and talents brought to organizations that utilize their volunteers well. Perhaps you have been a long-time volunteer for a not-for-profit organization. The volunteer work you do should reflect your own personal, professional, or career interest. If you are trained in the medical field, you may wish to support a hospital. If you are drawn to the cultural and performing arts, you would likely choose a volunteer path in these areas. Your enjoyment of your volunteer experience is tied closely to how seriously the organization values your time, effort, and expertise. Commitment to a cause may fade quickly when the organization does not acknowledge the importance of your volunteer effort.

It is not the outcomes of the organization's work alone that sustains loyalty. Volunteers seek a sense of community when they work for an organization. Volunteers must feel both wanted and useful. Most people's time is at a premium. You should expect to be treated fairly and honestly. For the most part, not-for-profit organizations have strong track records of working well with volunteers. However, be aware that some organizations are adept at talking about the need for volunteers, but cannot hold on to them, because they do not know how to use volunteers well. Also, organizations fail to think of volunteers as equal to, and colleagues of, the key administrative staff. Smaller organizations especially appreciate volunteers' time, and tend to nurture their interest. Volunteers who can give both time and money to the organization of their choice are a precious asset.

Helping Without Giving Money

The potential rewards are great when you help others through volunteer work. You learn new things. You interact with new people. You strengthen your own abilities. Ways to do so include helping with the infirm, the aged, working in a soup kitchen, or tutoring youth. Reading to the blind, delivering meals on wheels, giving blood, and staffing hospital gift shops and information desks are additional examples of ways to give your volunteer time. You can make a difference with small acts. Giving of one's time and effort has meaning totally separate from making a donation of money. Volunteering is appreciated. It is valued in American culture. You also come to know the organization at which you volunteer in a more intimate way, and note how it reflects your interests. It can give you interesting experiences to relate.

One example of a valuable volunteer service would be to become a Big Brother or Big Sister. In this role you serve as a role model for someone who might have few mentors, guides, or close relatives with whom to share the experiences of growing up.

Making Time to Volunteer

In two-parent households where both parents work giving volunteer time is generally more difficult, but still possible nonetheless. Those in this situation should choose an activity of mutual interest, so that each partner understands why, in addition to work, there should be time away from one another and family. If your children are old enough, explain to them about your volunteer time, why you are doing it and where. Ask them to join you in volunteering. Describe your experiences volunteering with your children to the rest of the family. By volunteering with your children you will be teaching them good habits for when they become adults.

Many people came into your life when you were growing up. Some of us may stay in touch with the people that have been most meaningful in our formative years long after we have moved away as adults. These people have made unforgettable impressions as a result of what they gave us of themselves.

Now we should try to make a similar impact in other people's lives. An appropriate image is that each of us, having received help from others, may take on the responsibility for rolling a hoop of caring and involvement along our chosen pathways for successive generations to later take on themselves.

Why U.S. Volunteers Are Special

Living in the new American democracy is unique, wrote French nobleman Alexis de Tocqueville. In 1803 he completed two years of travel and observation of our growing country. What impressed him most, beyond our youthful vigor, and our openness, was the size of the land (the Louisiana Purchase tripled our existing land mass, and was completed during his travels). He was amazed at Americans' willingness to volunteer. He marveled at the uniqueness of ordinary citizens who gave volunteer time to participate in Town Hall meetings. Citizens followed their own self-interests in giving volunteer time.

He was surprised that community meetings were open to everyone. De Tocqueville thought that organizing volunteer fire and police departments, and solving issues of governance for the public good by volunteers was not possible in Europe. He wrote that Europe was locked into its tradition of governance by kingships and feudal lords. In his view, because our society was not based on a class system, everyone had a chance to participate freely.

De Tocqueville's comments still hold fast today. We are a more mature democracy, but our level of volunteer involvement, and support of institutions by voluntary donations, is unparalleled anywhere else in the world. Our not-for-profit sector is the most advanced and sophisticated in the world. It extends well beyond our charitable institutions. Volunteer involvement forms the original basis for philanthropy, and is no longer limited to the social service networks. In the ebb and flow of government funding for activities in the not-for-profit sector, the role of volunteers is crucial. Even when you may think there is not enough time for volunteering, it is possible to do so for a few hours a week or a month.

As budgets shrink due to a decline in government funding, volunteers are the lifeblood of many organizations. Volunteers are utilized for their work, their advocacy, and public relations. They help raise money. Their connection to an organization gives it greater status and credibility. Americans look at who is attached to an organization, who serves on an organization board. They look to see who supports the organization when they receive campaign materials. These matters may well influence you as you give money away. You, who give time and money, are a major factor in the strength of America's not-for-profit sector.

An Agent to Make Change

For a donor to make social change happen is dependent on timing, the right leadership and implementing ideas. Sol Alinsky, a radical labor organizer of the 1950's and '60's on Chicago's Southwest Side found a handle to pull together small factions of workers, mostly of color, who lived near to the campus of the University of Chicago. These folks were tough, angry men who mostly labored in the city's stockyards. They carried a great deal of resentment toward the privileged students and administration. That world functioned within the confines of splendid Gothic buildings that lined the university's campus, while the surrounding neighborhood had deteriorated rapidly. The relative resources each group possessed were badly unbalanced. Using the persuasion of mutual self-interest, the University and the Back of the Yards worker group were brought together to form the Woodlawn Association. This unlikely alliance, engineered by Alinsky, provided a framework for social change. The Woodlawn Association was dedicated to improving the neighborhood for all concerned, with each population airing their concerns and grievances; then finding ways to seek solutions cooperatively. A great deal of volunteer time and money was placed into what was and continues today to be a successful urban model, bringing together dissimilar populations to co-exist with minimal conflict and maximum aid.

Change Not Always Possible

Funders must recognize that efforts to promote social change do not always succeed. A situation in a large junior high school in the Midwest illustrates this point. Here the principal's management style was highly authoritarian. The school PTA was not well-organized, and had minimal parent involvement. It was dominated by the principal's influence. The principal wanted to take almost all the funds collected in (not-for-profit) PTA dues to build a huge mounted sign bearing the school's name, to be positioned above the nearby interstate highway. The sign would be seen by motorists going in only one direction. A group of parents were aghast at the planned use of the PTA's funds. Having followed their children's classroom assignments, they knew that the school library lacked sufficient books, both in numbers and kinds of reading material. They wanted to spend the $850.00 PTA dues raised to strengthen the library holdings. Time was short and the group did not really know how to lobby the school's parents. The group agreed upon a strategy to present the library book purchase plan at the next PTA meeting. They planned to urge the need for a stronger library, by purchasing books with the money, hoping to effect social change for the school.

Two mothers from the group mounted the podium to present the book purchase plan. However, none of the small group's parents in the audience rose to endorse the book purchase plan. PTA representatives were not aware of, nor won over, to the group's plan. Instead, they endorsed the principal's wishes. Silence within the rest of the audience killed the idea for meaningful social change. The PTA parents did not understand or realize how more books could improve the library for their children. Parents often see a school principal as an authority figure. Clearly the small parent group had not taken the time to work out the conflict with him nor to convince leadership of the PTA. They were not sufficiently organized, and they lacked experience in knowing how to challenge an agenda that appeared already in place. This small parent group was immobilized, and was kept from being successful. Consequently, spending money for a better school library was voted down in favor of a freeway sign with the school's name on it.

To have achieved a desired social change, many forms of political behavior had to be understood, planned, and worked on before the PTA meeting took place. Compare the parents' weak organizing plan with the successful Woodlawn effort. Time, adequate preparation, lobbying and energizing others, and even luck, all contribute to successful social change. Enabling change by mobilizing a strong group effort is not easy. Donors make errors, just as businesses and individuals do. Success depends on many factors, including an organization's staff, knowledge, experience, courage, and funding sophistication. Sometimes a plan goes astray, or the timing is wrong. Intervening circumstances can prevent a program from being mounted successfully. Sometimes staff is inept. Or proper planning was not done. A project can fail simply because not enough financial support can be mobilized. Donors and volunteers need to accept that not every charitable gift or volunteer time they contribute to works out well, or accomplishes what it is meant to do.

One Person Enables Another

A founder and manager of a not-for-profit organization, who was responsible for the organization's success in obtaining oral histories of Holocaust survivors over a period of sixteen years, decided to return to university studies after a nineteen year absence to complete her advanced degree. Having run an organization and taught others about oral history techniques, Laura possessed strong writing skills and managed a medium-size budget as well. Lacking just a few credits, it appeared that finishing her degree would be simple. Not so. The university she contacted demanded that certain procedures be followed, procedures that to Laura seemed overly time-consuming and distracting. However, a friend volunteered to help out by mentoring her studying and writing. Having a personal cheerleader provided Laura with the confidence to follow the work protocol at the university. The mentor showed how it was possible to bend the degree requirements to fit Laura's interests. Consequently, a middle aged student realized that attaining her Ph.D. was possible after all.

Funding the Arts Differently

The San Francisco Voluntary Arts Fund is a good example of how funding the arts differently can provide opportunities for many local residents to enjoy outdoor concerts and other performances. San Francisco residents have the option of contributing to this fund with their year-end property taxes. Taxpayers are given additional motivation to give by the fact that cultural arts donations are tax deductible. The Voluntary Arts Fund has changed cultural arts in the city. Small arts groups are encouraged to present their ideas and materials. Dependency on government funds and donations from foundations, companies, and individuals are no longer the only sources of support for the city's cultural arts programming. As federal funding for the arts has become severely limited, this discrete Voluntary Arts Fund allows citizens of all ages to enjoy wonderful arts events. Because funding has been cut from the National Endowment for the Arts to almost nothing, the Voluntary Arts Fund is crucial to the quality of cultural life in San Francisco. By joining with others, even modest donations help sustain the quality of civic life in the community. Each donor thus enables many other people to enjoy the city's cultural arts. This kind of fund can be replicated in other communities regardless of size. Voluntary funding, together with volunteer time given by citizens, are the particular hallmarks of American life that De Tocqueville noted almost two hundred years ago.

Many donors may want to move away from funding charitable organizations engaged in delivering direct social services. Yet the need for social services always continues to be great. The elderly, newcomers to America, and a growing underclass of Americans all receive less help from government. Too many support systems have been dismantled or had their funding severely diminished. Still, empowering others with private charitable dollars is possible.

Fixing Society's Problems

Is it possible to solve the whole range of problems that continue to appear in the news, as well as those hidden from view? Will there ever be sufficient low-cost affordable housing? Will welfare recipients be able to become independent, long-term job-holders through education and job training? Will the effects of drug and alcohol abuse always plague us? Will family and child abuse ever end? Will there always be a homeless population? Are we free from taking on our small portion of these large tasks? No, not if we want our world to make the lives of the less fortunate better. Not if we ourselves want to live in a healthy society.

These issues are before us. The solutions appear distant, difficult, and unattainable. Such massive problems are national, widespread, and serious. But by taking a smaller look within one's own community, it is possible to focus on a single problem and involve oneself in seeking solutions. Your volunteer time and financial help do make a difference. It may be that you provide help to the sick, the elderly, the abused, the chemically dependent, the homeless, or the AIDS sufferers. For those concerned with First Amendment issues of protecting religion, speech, and press freedom there are a host of organizations that welcome your assistance.

Are we free from taking on our small portion of these large tasks? No, not if we want our world to make the lives of the less fortunate better. Not if we ourselves want to live in a healthy society. In American democracy, watchful citizens try to ensure the protection of both our Constitution and the Bill of Rights. At the end of each year, you can look over what you have done and evaluate your charitable involvement. If someone is better off than they were before your volunteer time and donations, you are helping to repair our world. Problems solved are replaced by new problems. Your personal attention to philanthropic acts of giving do matter. They can make a difference.

Charitable Giving and Entertainment

For people who do not like to become involved in the more weighty problems facing society, there is the lighter side, including support of sports teams, the arts, and social events that hold fundraising efforts. These events are designed as a way to attract support for a given organization. Often the donor does not respond first and foremost to the merits of the organization and its mission. Donors respond to who is asking for support, and what reward, or exchange, comes with the gift. For your donation, you may receive complimentary tickets to a show, sporting event, or a dinner. You may receive an award, a gift, or prize. The IRS, however, only allows partial deductions for the price of meals served at an event. So if a ticket cost is set at, say, $150, fifty dollars may represent the cost of food. You are allowed to deduct the other $100 as your charitable gift.

Donors Like Exchanges

Exchanges given in return for support of an organization's project have merit. They provide tangible evidence of appreciation for your gift. They also provide a pleasant memory of your organizational attachment. Some donors like to be allowed to be seen at a public event, as showing support for an organization, even if they know very little about it. The social motivation is high. Additionally, some donors may enjoy being given the opportunity to introduce friends and family to the charitable organization they are involved with. Be aware that if you, as a donor, invite others to what is perceived as your cause, those invited may wish to invite you, in return, to support their cause.

There are other types of exchanges between donors and charitable institutions. Some examples of things charitable institutions give back to donors in exchange for gifts include invitations to hear a special speaker, receptions, informal gatherings and galas, followed up by both written and verbal acknowledgment of your support. Some organizations present certificates as thanks for your support. Others "romance" their funders by calling them to bring them up to date on what is going on, or again to thank them for ongoing support in between fundraising campaigns. You may receive printed matter, books, pamphlets, and photographs. These contacts are all designed to make sure you do not forget the organization that you are supporting, and to keep your focus on future support.

For some donors, exchanges are expected and enjoyed; others are indifferent to rewards. Many families are proud of being part of service clubs, like Rotary, Links, or Kiwanis. Virtually everyone appreciates being acknowledged for their contribution, whether monetary, volunteer time, or both. The desire to be socially recognized for one's contributions to philanthropy has a long tradition in our culture.

Chapter IX

Perspectives on Giving

Funders in Relationships With Their Charities

Think of a receiving organization as the other half of your dynamic relationship in the process of charitable giving. The older notion of charitable giving with donor in the role of "do gooder," or angel, does not apply any longer. Your contribution is based upon your understanding and interest in a particular organization's vision and operation. Express your commitment with money that enables the organization to do its work. Together, you are helping meet strategic goals. The underlying rationale of your gift is to contribute to the organization's performance. To keep the relationship vibrant, organizations need to communicate that they are using your money in a productive manner. Most organizations understand this and follow suit. You will most likely find the more active communication between donors and their charities common today to be satisfying.

The Importance of Timing

Philanthropy usually makes the news only when the gift is a large sum of money, or there is an unusual circumstance connected to the gift. Two recent news-worthy events in philanthropy that fit these bills involved an elderly African-American laundress, Oseola McCarty. She labored hard for decades, living most frugally, in order to put aside her life savings of $150,000. She wanted to give away her money to provide a college scholarship for a young black woman, who could obtain higher education, an opportunity denied Ms. McCarty. Inspired by Ms. McCarty's powerful commitment, although for entirely different reasons, CNN media mogul Ted Turner reviewed his abundant assets and pledged a gift of $1,000,000,000—yes, one billion dollars—to help strengthen the work of the United Nations. The magnitude of Turner's gift, and the relative largesse of the McCarty gift are unusual experiences in charitable giving.

There are profound differences between these two gifts that go beyond the size of each donor's individual act of philanthropy. One difference is that Ms. McCarty worked an entire lifetime, skimping and saving dollars all the while, in order to enable an unknown young woman to receive a scholarship for higher education. She wanted to let another woman move forward with more education to make something of herself in life. Mr. Turner's billion dollar gift is not the first generous act of philanthropy that this major benefactor has bestowed, nor is it the last of which he is capable. Another difference between these two impressive gifts is that Ms. McCarty's gift of setting up an education scholarship is specific. Mr. Turner's gift is general, for the purpose of alleviating the budget deficits of the United Nations organization. Both donor acts received national publicity and acknowledgment. How effective these acts of charitable giving will be in the life of the scholarship recipients, in one case, or in the future the United Nations, in the other case, remains to be evaluated in the future.

Both gifts were given in a timely manner. Ms. McCarty is aging, and schools and colleges are happy to receive scholarship funds to assist able, young African-American men and women. The United Nations budget has been suffering from the lack of dues payments assessed the United States. Both donors have been thoughtful about when and how to do their acts of philanthropy.

You can think and act globally, as did Mr. Turner, or you can set your sights on a local project, close to home. Ms. McCarty gave her money as a reflection of her personal life history, wanting to help someone nearby. Close to home gifts may include the local chapter of a large national organization, such as the Humane Society, your local food bank or scouting organization. You have choices for giving near or far for very small or very sizable gifts.

Strength of Targeted Giving

Using philanthropic funds from business, James Barksdale, former president of Netscape Communications, and his wife, Sally, gave $100 million to promote the teaching of reading in their home state of Mississippi, which has the lowest literacy rate in the U.S.

By carefully targeting their philanthropic gift, the Barksdales determined to make an impact, and hopefully a difference, in the reading achievement of children. Furthermore, they chose to place their money in the state where both Barksdales attended college at the University of Mississippi. This gift marks one of the five largest donations by private individuals or foundations to a public university. Obviously, this family considered carefully the potential strength of their large, targeted gift.

Thinking About Philanthropy

Being of moderate means does not exclude you from practicing philanthropy. Only a small portion of the population has huge dollars in income and assets. Many people set up a pattern early in life of sharing their time and their money. Volunteering also continues to be an important form of giving, as has been discussed earlier.

Significant amounts of earned income are donated annually to not-for-profit organizations, mostly in small increments. Some examples follow to illustrate how small, regular donations continue to reinforce areas of philanthropic choice. Perhaps you remember putting change or dollars into the collection plate at Sunday morning church services. Perhaps you set up a lemonade stand, and used the sale proceeds to help your school. Thus, you received early lessons about giving, and knew the recipients directly. Maybe you worked voluntarily to sell subscriptions for your school or college newspaper, trying to raise money for its budget. Such volunteer work cost you time, effort, and money you might have earned at other paid work. You might have used this time and effort for personal pursuits, for sports activities, study, or sleep. All these examples indicate how you can make a charitable contribution, with money, time, and effort. These acts are cumulative and become significant when multiplied by other people doing the same things. Jointly, they constitute the way philanthropy works on a daily basis across America.

Adults Manage Giving

During your young adult years, your earnings are likely to increase. If you marry and have children, you are likely to incur long term expenses, such as a home mortgage and the costs of schools, camps, and lessons for your children. Single people have expenses also, and may be even less involved with community concerns. Perhaps you have to help out a close relative, or have unexpected health expenses to deal with. Should you wish to make charitable contributions, they may be modest and limited to few selected organizations. The wish to give may be present, but your financial resources are slim for philanthropy.

However, people do make occasional charitable gifts within their limited means when they are younger. Some people choose to be church members, engage in political activism, or an athletic activity that requires support by membership. As the *Giving USA* chart in Chapter V illustrated, after giving to religious and religiously supported organizations, Americans prefer to support institutions from which they received their education, or support education-related activities.

Few people plan ahead for their future charitable giving, but you should begin now. Research shows that most gifts of size are made in the last year of a person's life.

Giving will probably change over your life as a donor, reflecting changes in interests and life styles. Older parents and grandparents support the causes and schools that their family is involved with. The ongoing transfer of intergenerational wealth over the next two decades amounts to trillions of dollars. It affects populations locally and nationally, and even internationally. Giving money away, and doing it effectively, is a lifetime pursuit for donors of all ages.

Obtaining Information About Giving

Keeping abreast of what is going on in the field of philanthropy is helpful for managing your giving. Philanthropic activities are reported through *Foundation News Magazine,* which is mailed to all members of the Council on Foundations. In addition to the *Chronicle of Philanthropy*'s on-line service, one can subscribe to the service's biweekly newspaper to get thorough reportage about charitable activities, job opportunities, and features about special philanthropists and foundations. Through annual reports, brochures, articles, and news releases, philanthropic grants of significance are made known to the public. If you live in a city with a Foundation Center, you can visit the Center and thereby learn about particular not-for-profit organizations. Your public library is also a source of information about not-for-profits. As noted in Chapter VII, some not-for-profit organizations have an Internet presence that you can access. In the "Resources" section in the back of the book, you will find contact information concerning organizations that service donors.

The Internet is used in a particular way by a limited number of philanthropic organizations. These organizations working together are similar to a community foundation, and operate as a sort of mutual fund. The idea is that you write a check to the Internet organization, which, in turn, disburses funds by making grants to charities of the type you prefer and designate. So far, this medium has not been particularly successful at attracting donors. It may seem too remote to be a worthy activity for those wishing to give away money. It leaves the choices of giving to people far away, whom you do not know, who select charities you may not know either. Some of those soliciting support have been caught embezzling some of the money.

However, annual reports, brochures, articles, news releases, and philanthropic grants of significance are constantly being made public. Often community foundations have information about organizations that they are willing to share. In general, you have to pursue your funding interests by doing your own research.

Saying No

It is okay to say no when you are asked to support an organization. However, it can be hard to say no if your best friend or close relative asks. If you are in conflict between your head and your heart about making a gift, listen to your heart. If you have no interest in the receiving organization for your own reasons, your response can be that you will help this one time only, because of the person who is asking you. If you have already supported an organization for a long time, it is okay to ask for time off. Let others now lend support and have the organization no longer rely on your help, at least for the time being. If you have already decided on a focus for giving, it is much easier to tell anybody who asks for assistance "no." Be truthful and explain that you are sure their work is worthwhile, but you have other plans for giving away your money.

You need to indicate to an organization if you have shifted your giving priorities, or if your financial situation does not permit continued support. Drop-offs in charitable support are understood and accepted with good grace by most organizations. If you have been a longtime supporter, most organizations will acknowledge your past giving with thanks. If you have been regularly giving a thousand dollars or more to an organization, it is harder for the not-for-profit to fill quickly the monetary gap your donation represents, especially if the not-for-profit is small and new. Try to phase down your gift over two, or even three years. Ideally, your leave-taking is understood by both yourself and the receiving organization, without a sense of disappointment and/or guilt on either part.

Bricks vs. Program Services

In the not-for-profit sector both capital expenditures and program services are important. One appeal is as worthwhile as the other. Donors are able to visualize and understand more readily what a new wing for a building or what new science and computer equipment will look like. How a scholarship program will be shaped, or what will be the effect of an after school program for youth is harder to visualize and to measure. If you are the kind of person who does not relate well to program costs, regardless of subject matter, then your philanthropy may be better geared towards something tangible and concrete. If you are interested in investing your charitable funds in educating people, or running a direct service program, then you are more likely to be attracted to requests for program and services funding.

In supporting a new building project, you need to ask why the capital campaign is taking place. Find out if funds for staffing and programs are also in place. You should ask also if there are reserve funds set up to take care of the new structure, or to replace obsolete equipment. Plans for a new structure may look attractive on paper, but must result in practical application to meet the purposes for which money is being raised. Whether you are donating money for merely one brick, or for a large piece of the capital project, the issues of adequate funds for staffing, furnishings, and ongoing maintenance should be answered to your satisfaction.

Why Anonymous Gifts

In reading a donor list of support to an organization, you may occasionally see a listing of an anonymous gift. What is the reason for giving money this way? In a situation of family tension between adult siblings, and/or parents, an anonymous gift by one sibling and spouse is a way of having to avoid explanations to the rest of the family for their philanthropic choice. A respected community member gave an anonymous challenge grant to the board of an organization she had once chaired. Her reasoning was that the board was undergiving in relation to its capacity, stated commitment to give, and its willingness to ask others for help. The anonymous grant required a match from board members on a two to one basis. The board had the choice of raising all the matching funds among its own members, or going out into the community to ask for support of the organization's work. By giving anonymously, this donor avoided possible resentment on the part of the board members if they had learned the source of the gift. If they had learned that she was the contributor they might have discerned her implicit criticism of the board.

The most outstanding instance of anonymous giving in America came recently when it was discovered that Mr. James Feeney, a co-founder of Duty Free Shops, had given well over six million dollars to various not-for-profits, using his attorney and a dummy foundation as intermediary. This man wanted his philanthropy to be thoughtful, quiet, unassuming, and without any requirement for the not-for-profits to give him any kind of acknowledgment or publicity.

Resolving Conflicts in Society

Significant charitable giving is aimed at resolving conflicts in society. Numerous human relations and human rights organizations are dedicated to social and educational work to help people get along better with one another. Key organizations working in conflict resolution include the American Friends Service Committee, the Anti-Defamation League, and the Arab Anti-Defamation League. These organizations promote education as the way to diffuse conflict. Some organizations seek to resolve conflicts by legal recourse, either to protect aggrieved parties, or to mount a defense when discussion has not resolved a problem. Groups such as the Environmental Defense Fund, Earthworks, and the National Partnership for Women and Children are examples of such groups.

Advocacy Groups Without Deductions

Advocacy groups also deal with contentious issues. Citizen groups do battle against an arm of local or national government. For instance, in California, propositions appear on ballots regularly, around which advocacy groups rally. Measures to end affirmative action or to ban smoking in restaurants illustrate this kind of activity.

Some organizations do intensive governmental lobbying. Lobbying is a legitimate activity under the Constitution, but not all organizations which do this work can offer tax deductibility for donations. Investigate whether your gift to a lobbying organization is deductible, according to the federal tax code. Not-for-profit organizations, to which gifts are all tax deductible, are limited to spending no more that 5% of their budget on lobbying. Even without deductibility, donors write checks anyway, because they believe in the work accomplished by lobbying organizations, and are willing to forego the tax benefit of supporting a not-for-profit organization. Mentally, donors may think of their check as a charitable donation, but it is really a donation for the purpose of lobbying.

Protecting Others' Rights

Protecting the rights of those who are not fully able to protect themselves has always been a motivating factor behind much charitable giving. This sort of motivation lies behind some of the giving to groups concerned with animal rights, the rights of illegal aliens, or the welfare of the mentally retarded.

Using a combination of charitable dollars linked with legislative measures before bodies of government, people are willing to show their commitment to special interest issues. Efforts are made to raise public awareness through education with print and Internet educational materials. Action is linked to education by means of public demonstrations, media statements, and getting voters to respond to advocacy measures on the ballot. Often not-for-profit and lobbying organizations join forces and work in collaboration. An example of the success of this sort of effort is the federally mandated Clean Water and Air Act. It was achieved by combining the political strength of large membership groups such as the Environmental Defense Fund, The Nature Conservancy, and The Sierra Club.

Local organizations in large states like California have proven their effectiveness in preserving open space by means of not-for-profit trusts, like the Peninsula Open Space Trust. Such organizations buy up land that would otherwise go for home or commercial development. Friends of the River lobbies and promotes legislation to keep rivers from being dammed, wishing to preserve their natural state for fishing and recreation. The citizens' Mono Lake Committee came into existence to battle the Los Angeles Public Water District by successfully going to court twice, forcing the district to restore water that it was systematically draining out of the lake to give agriculture and residential water consumers in the Los Angeles area cheap water rates. This unique Sierra mountain lake developed dangerously low water levels with accompanying despoliation of its ecosystem. It was citizen participation giving volunteer time for advocacy and lobbying, together with charitable contributions, that saved this pristine mountain lake, and restored its water to a safe level for nature and tourists.

The Headwaters old growth redwood trees battle involved the state of California, the federal government, and environmental groups dealing with a large private corporation over the corporation's cutting down of giant trees over two thousand years of age. The issue has been settled temporarily, by buying the Headwaters grove from the lumber company, and permitting cutting of other redwoods on a restricted basis. Not-for-profit groups played a vital role in helping write protective legislation to preserve the ancient redwoods and the animal life that flourishes in these forests. This example of lobbying, legislation, and affinity group action, working together with the government, shows how effective your own philanthropic participation may be to advance specific interests.

Chapter X

Uniqueness of Personal Philanthropy

Philanthropy Addresses Needs

The role of those giving money away is to address needs in society. These are needs that the government, local and national, is not remedying, or not remedying sufficiently. The not-for-profit organizations try to address what government cannot accomplish and does not participate in doing. With the recent cutbacks in federal funding for not-for-profits, there is a greater need than before for individual contributions to these not-for-profits. Charities hope that the voluntary sector will be able to plug the holes that resulted in decreased funding. At this time, data shows that voluntary giving is not making up for the dramatic withdrawal of public tax money. Units of government, whether local, state, or federal all play a role in assisting with funding of social services. Decreased federal funding means that the independent sector has to rely on other government levels for assistance, increased individual contributions, or suffer severe cutbacks in helping others.

Has charitable giving become just like business? Is it becoming a business too complex for ordinary people to assist with and comprehend? To give sensible answers to these questions, let us think of philanthropy as a special and separate subject. It is a field of its own, just as we consider sports separate from fine arts, or history separate from commerce. There are definite connections between each philanthropic subject, and even some overlaps. Yet, we need to consider what philanthropy involves and why it deserves our attention. It is a valuable part of America's gross national product. The not-for-profit sector produces many jobs, and spends donated money for goods and services throughout the economy. Philanthropy occupies a legitimate place in your daily endeavors.

Is Philanthropy a Business?

Giving money away is a kind of business, similar in many ways to, but still very separate from, for-profit enterprises. There is no "bottom line," the well known expression for making a profit. All publicly held companies are dependent upon stockholder approval and satisfaction. Like publicly held companies, not-for-profits are required to fill out a (990 form) tax return, and are therefore open to public scrutiny. The need to show black ink, or profits, is usually integral to doing business. Losing money for any length of time is unacceptable. Though not-for-profits also need to be financially responsible—break even—they have their own version of a "bottom line." It is cast not in dollar profits made, but in matters such as services rendered, goals reached, problems solved, learning and research accomplished, and crises averted or met successfully. These kinds of achievements are certainly worthy of respect on their own terms. As funder, you need to have useful tools for asking about such "bottom line" goals. If you give volunteer time, that is also a way to be involved in the "business" of the not-for-profit sector.

You can learn about the general work of any charitable organization by asking the right questions. Making a personal connection to a not-for-profit you have interest in gives you satisfaction that your money and knowledge are being integrated well.

Philanthropic Organizations and You

Your potential gift makes you important for an organization. It is in their self-interest to make themselves available. Your own understanding of its work, of getting to know staff and organizational activity, will lead you to feel more confident about making a gift. To engage your attention and obtain repeat support from funders, organizations release reports on their work and future plans annually. Keeping a funder's attention on the organization, hopefully for continuing and increased support, is mandatory for all not-for-profit organizations to stay in business.

The "hands on" approach to funding is not always possible, so your next best course is to rely on others whose judgment you value. You may talk with friends, associates, and relatives who do support the entity you are considering. The organization that you are considering giving your help to may be well known nationally, or have a strong, established reputation locally. Sometimes the print press covers the work of the organization to which you are considering support. Word of mouth approval is one way that not-for-profits know that their vision and performance is well accepted by funders. If you are invited to an event sponsored by the organization, you can talk with other attendees and find out why they like this not-for-profit.

Think Through Your Gift

Be clear about why you wish to make a gift, and what you hope to accomplish. Think through whether there is a single or several reasons to give philanthropy in each instance. Is it a "paying back" gift for help received? Is it to help out in a crisis situation? Is it a gift in response to someone who asks you for a donation, even though the subject matter does not normally interest you, but you feel a business or social relationship requires your response? Is it an area that touches your life, and already has your charitable involvement? Is the company you work for one that matches your charitable giving? Do you feel that you are doing the right thing, being socially responsible, by donating? These are just some of the questions that may arise when you, your spouse, partner, or your family consider charitable choices. A "yes" answer to any one of these questions is a perfectly acceptable basis for your decisions regarding philanthropy.

Author Claude Rosenberg, in his book on philanthropy, *Wealthy and Wise,* makes an economic argument for giving gifts on a current basis and not waiting until later. The analogy he uses to explain why current giving is better, is that the charitable dollar buys more today, just as the fancy ball gown that you bought twelve years ago would cost approximately twice as much if bought today. In other words, each given dollar now is more valuable than it will be in a few years, when price inflation has diminished its purchasing power. In philanthropy, you are the consumer. You are purchasing an opportunity to support, with cash or equities, a charitable product produced by the organization of your choice. The Rosenberg argument is aimed at people of large giving capacity, but the principles still hold for anyone's charitable gift program.

Philanthropy is Cause-Driven

In his article, "Mixed Motives" in *The American Benefactor,* Mark Kramer says that all charitable giving may be categorized three ways—social, obligatory, and strategic. Giving socially is when one gives when asked to by a relative, friend, or business associate. Obligatory giving arises from a sense of duty to one's community, whether it be a church/synagogue, geographic, or special interest group of people with common interests. Strategic giving is quite different. These kinds of gifts are motivated by a personal commitment and desire to become involved with an organization based on your interest, enthusiasm, knowledge, etc. In strategic giving, you want to make a gift based on doing something personally meaningful that will matter to both the funder and the organization.

How you give away money says more about you as a person than how you made it, according to Gary Wexler, a public relations specialist with not-for-profit clients. His lectures on "passion marketing" stress that money itself does not know about caring and concern, religion, love, or commitment. Our society often accords recognition to people who are successful, with the measure of success being the money you earn. Just as making money requires professional discipline, thinks Wexler, so does giving it away. When you are a philanthropist, you are buying in with your soul, wanting to be a better person, make the world better, by giving both your time and your money. This is a deep commitment that can be both strategic and fun.

People who consider themselves capable in whatever they do professionally need to break through the myths and fears that giving money away is hard to do. Making an error in the field in which you work seems more acceptable than in philanthropy, in which you do not have immediate proficiency. Becoming a philanthropist is a step-by-step process of making choices that reflect your personal values and concerns. Your ability to be in control is not the desired outcome. The outcome needs to be mutual satisfaction between funder and recipient, so that both think they have accomplished their tasks: one to ask for help needed; the other to respond to the request for support with a gift. Remember that you are giving a gift of your own choice, no matter if the motivation is one of three categories mentioned—obligatory, social, or strategic.

Managing Voluntary Giving

Giving away money is a personal act. It may be done solo, or with a partner or group of partners. It is a voluntary act. You may or may not enjoy giving away money, but you can surely become a more effective funder, one who develops funding skills, and achieves a higher level of competence. Writing checks in itself does not make you an effective funder. But engaging in philanthropy with your heart, involvement, and commitment make your efforts one of passion. This is your cause, your work, and your desire. A few of your choices are likely to produce frustration, because you cannot evaluate the effect of your gift, or you feel that it is not being used well or for what purpose you intended. Learning comes from failures, or more properly stated, from disappointment in your giving decision. In the course of becoming a more effective funder you cannot always be completely pleased.

As a donor, you may be asked to serve on the board of an organization you have chosen to support. Many people recoil from this invitation to serve, claiming they do not know enough about being a board member. Actually, you need most to understand the process of being a board member. The organization's operations will become more evident to you as you serve through your term. It is important that you ask any organization whose board you are considering serving on what their expectations are of you. In turn, you should expect the following things from the organization: an orientation experience for new members of the board; timely notice of meetings; budgets that are easily understandable; and the ability to call and ask questions and make comments about whatever else you wish to know. Board service can be interesting and personally rewarding.

In business, the market responds to a service or product being offered. In philanthropy, you are being offered a cause, a mission, a work in progress. Products and services may also be offered. The separate characteristics noted above are what distinguishes a not-for-profit activity from entrepreneurial enterprises. Below you will find ways in which to measure your effectiveness as a funder of not-for-profit activity.

You Can Be a More Effective Funder

Here are ten important rules for being a more effective funder:

1. *Know that philanthropy is a big subject,* growing and diverse. It is a dynamic activity, with the potential for many positive outcomes. You will learn about philanthropy through your experiences giving to philanthropic organizations. You may select your own particular area of philanthropic interest. Discussions with your spouse or partner, and the rest of your family helps to clarify what is your major area of concern. You do have to want to make a difference by making a gift.

2. *As you gain successes in giving away your money, gain confidence in your choices.* It is a challenging and fun activity, one of passionate involvement. Philanthropy is a voluntary act, with a religious and/or ethical basis. The religious underpinnings are related to biblical mandates about taking care of others. Thus you may apply the moral lessons you learned when you were very young from your family. They include helping and concern for others, sharing with the less fortunate, and being compassionate about social needs and problems. Today, Americans understand that funds raised by the third, or voluntary, sector augment and sustain thousands of worthwhile organizations that run the gamut of activity in society.

3. *Anyone can learn about philanthropy.* You do not have to be an expert to make an effective donation decision. Philanthropy involves many processes and steps that lead to the act of giving. These processes are not mysterious. Funders must remember that the grantee organization receiving your gift is your partner, and the organization must consider you, the funder, also as their partner. Think through the purpose of your gift, know as much as possible about your chosen charity, and determine what you want to accomplish with your gift. Then evaluate your gift afterward to test its effectiveness.

4. *Gift size alone does not define effective philanthropy.* You can provide important help with modest funding, especially to new and small organizations, and even to large institutions with a national funding base.

5. *There is no one right way to do your philanthropy.* Effective funders should investigate how others are dealing with their issues of interest and concern. Find out what else is working well, and what is not. If you are not able physically to visit the organization of your choice, but can keep up by phone, Internet, e-mail, and postal mail with what is going on, that is fine. Otherwise, there is no substitute for actually knowing who is running an organization and visiting to follow up on their work. As a donor, you are entitled to as much information as you wish to seek.

6. *Practice improves how you think and act* respecting a donation decision. It may not make you perfect, but your confidence develops the more you undertake donation decisions. There emerges a pattern that can work for you, such as focus on health or education issues, ones about social justice, or children's services. You can learn a great deal from errors and oversights, from reading about the charities, and from talking with other funders, and with the staff of the organization you are involved with, or are considering supporting.

7. *Think about what you desire to support,* and what is motivating you. Recall what you have funded in the past, what your pattern has

been, or what pattern you want to establish. Each year you should consider listing your annual gifts according to the priority you assign them. Try to analyze what gifts have given you the most positive feeling, and which giving experiences have been less than satisfactory. Consider why certain funding situations worked well, and which ones were unsatisfactory. Reflect on which gifts seemed to make the most difference to the organization you helped.

8. *Keep records of what you have given away.* Whether you use a computer or hand-written entries to record charitable donations, you must keep track of donation requests. File organizational materials, donations given, donation thank-you letters received, and any evaluations made. Back up this material on the computer. Make notes by writing a few paragraphs about what you gave money for, how much, when, and why. Relate the circumstances of involvement with your chosen not-for-profit. How did you come to your donation decision? Was it successful in meeting your expectations? If not, explain what happened and why. Be sure to save letters of thanks that you received in a file for at least five years in case there is an inquiry about your tax deductions. Some of the most memorable grants made are the ones that did not work out well. They serve to flag what to do differently next time a philanthropic decision is required.

9. *Have your philanthropy ordered in a file system.* You must manage your paper flow. What system you develop depends on whether you are doing the work yourself or with someone to help you. It is important to avoid piling up or misplacing requests pending your investigation as to whether you wish to give a gift. You need separate files for: requests for assistance; information gathered about a particular area of philanthropy, i.e. medicine or education; grants organized by date, grantee, amount, or how paid, i.e. cash, check, sale of securities or bonds; and material concerning matching funds from an employer. Decide if you plan to itemize gifts annually for tax reporting. Gifts should be organized by type and category, i.e., repeat gifts, annual, one-time, operating, honoring a person, etc. If it is a

multiyear pledge, enter the date and amount of each payment. By logging your gifts, you create a history of your own philanthropy. For persons involved in a family foundation, with two or more participants, compare gifts made annually with the foundation's mission statement of purpose, together with its funding guidelines.

10. *Encourage others to give.* Encourage your partner or spouse and family, friends, and associates to share their funding experiences so that you may compare and learn more, each of you obtaining a broader perspective of the subject. You can rejoice together about what you have funded that worked out well. You can also laugh about what went wrong with gifts that were not as successful.

Be Open to Change

It is appropriate to switch one's focus from one societal need to another, as these needs change around you. For example, homelessness has become a major concern in smaller as well as larger urban communities, and strategies for addressing the problems are still evolving, as we come to understand the problems that homeless people face. People change their focus of giving, because they think one area or organization has received, or is receiving, sufficient support. Once a vaccine was developed and put into use all over America, the indices of polio almost disappeared, and donors turned their attention and their gifts to other health issues.

People's philanthropic interests usually change over time. Funders may become more willing to take funding risks. They may realize that their gift is for a new purpose, a small, struggling not-for-profit or for a pilot project that may or may not become a significant funding program area. Some funders narrow their interests to one subject, like breast cancer research. Some wish to fund only local projects in or near to their home community, such as their church-sponsored activities.

You should expect both recognition and thanks for gifts of time or money or both. Organizations should tend to all donors, regardless of gift size. What begins as a modest gift, may, over time, become a major commitment on your part. Alternately, you may shift your areas of funding, as you think a particular issue requires more support. Successful charitable organizations realize the value of donor loyalty and commitment, and do excellent jobs in acknowledging gifts. Information flow to funders helps sustain interest. It increases donor understanding and appreciation of the work being done. Many donors judge the worth of a not-for-profit more for how they are treated as donors, than for any other objective measure. Personal relationships are often more valued than tasks accomplished or programs executed effectively and efficiently. The "care and feeding" of a donor may be the major reason why you continue to give your money to a given organization.

Recipe for Good Decision Making

You will find below ten basic ingredients for effective charitable decision making:

1. Know your area of philanthropic interest.
2. Become familiar with the organization(s) you want to support.
3. Tell the organization what you like and what concerns you about their work.
4. Feel free to ask an organization questions you want answered.
5. Talk to others, if possible, about the organization for more information and to learn about their experiences.
6. When you decide to make a gift, be clear whether it is for one time only, or if you expect to give regular support.
7. Think of yourself as making an investment in an organization's vision.
8. If the charity is a membership organization, participate and enjoy what it offers.
9. If the charity is not a membership organization, keep up with its work and goals.
10. Tell others proudly what you are doing; philanthropy is a well-kept secret!

You As a Philanthropist

Charitable giving can be learned, improved upon, enjoyed throughout one's lifetime. How you view your role as giver, donor, or funder—whatever term you prefer—is your personal choice. What money you determine to give is a reflection of your personality and mindset. This book has tried to help frame a generally little known subject in ways that give you working tools for making decisions. You will have a different awareness of philanthropy. Media stories on the subject will likely attract your attention. You may even find yourself talking about philanthropy at a cocktail party! At the end of your year's philanthropic effort, only you can assess what the giving experience has meant, both for yourself and for those with whom you are involved. You can be a successful funder and enjoy the process. Ideally, you can come away with warm and positive feelings about giving your money away!

Bibliography

Arenson, Karen. "Charity Giving in U.S. Rose 11% in '98. Says Report." *The New York Times* (May 26, 1999): A26.

Berkowitz, Leonard, and J.R. Macaulay, eds. *The Self, Selfishness and Altruism.* New York: Academic Press, 1970.

Carnegie, Andrew. *The Gospel of Wealth.* Rev. ed. Cambridge: Harvard University Press, Belknap Press, 1962.

Clotfelder, Charles T. *Federal Tax Policy and Charitable Giving.* Chicago: University Press, 1985.

Collier, Charles. *Planned Giving Today* (Nov. 1998): 3-4.

Cook, W. Bruce. "The Psychology of Investing." *Fund Raising Management* (March 1998): 13-16.

Dickey, Marilyn, and Marchettik Domenica. "A Giving Boom." *The Chronicle of Philanthropy* (June 3, 1999): 26-28.

Frank, Robert. *Giving.* p. 135-38.

Kaplan, Ann E., ed. *Giving, USA.* New York: AAFRC Trust for Philanthropy, 1998.

Kramer, Mark. "Mixed Motives." *The American Benefactor* (Winter 1998): 91-2.

Maimonides, Moses. *The Guide of the Perplexed.* Translated by Schlomo Pines. Chicago: University of Chicago Press, 1963.

Newman, Raquel H. "Perception of Factors Relating to Gender Differences in Philanthropy." Ph.D. diss., University of San Francisco, 1995.

Rosenberg, Claude, Jr. *Wealthy & Wise.* Boston: Little Brown and Co., 1994.

Schverish, Paul, and John J. Havens. "Daily Bread." *Findings from the First Diary Study on Giving & Volunteering*. 1996.

Tocqueville, Alexis de. *Democracy in America*. New York: A. A. Knopf, 1966.

Wexler, Gary. "Passion Marketing." Lecture presented at . . . , New York, fall 1998.

Wuthnow, Robert, and Virginia A. Hodgkinson. *Faith and Philanthropy in America*. San Francisco: Jossey-Bass Publishers, 1990.

Philanthropy Resources and Contact Information

Association of Small Foundations
4905 Del Rey Avenue, Suite 308
Bethesda, MD 20814
Phone: 301 907-3337 or 800 212-9922
E-mail: asf@erols.com   Website: www.SmallFoundations.org

A membership association for foundations with little or no staff, providing services to its members. Members volunteer to talk with other members about management, purchase of equipment and software, etc. Website has a members-only section with much useful information.

Center for the Study of Philanthropy
365 Fifth Avenue, 5th Floor
New York, NY 10016-4309
Phone: 212 817-2010 Fax: 212 817-1572

Has a newsletter. Focus on women in philanthropy. Catalog of publications.

Chronicle of Philanthropy
1255 23rd Street NW
Washington, DC 20037
Phone:202 466-1000 Fax: 202 466-2078
Website: www.philanthropy.com

A biweekly newspaper with articles about philanthropy, announcement of meetings on the subject, listing of selected grants given; ads for positions in the not-for-profit sector. Has an Internet resources page with links galore.

Council on Foundations
1828 L Street NW Suite 300
Washington, DC 20036-5168
Phone: 202 466-6512   Fax: 202 835-2993
E-mail: webmaster@cof.org   Website: www.cof.org

National membership organization providing a range of philanthropic information. Has large, annual conference and smaller conference for family foundations.

The Forum of Regional Associations of Grantmakers
1828 L Street NW, Suite 300
Washington, DC 20036
Phone: 202 467-0385
E-mail: forum@rag.org   Website: www.rag.org

RAGs have been formed in most parts of the country and serve as the central planning body for many philanthropic activities and resources in the region. RAGs organize and sponsor programs on a variety of topics.

The Foundation Center
79 5th Avenue (at 16th Street)
New York, NY 10003-3076
Phone: 212 620-4230 Fax: 212 807-3677
Website: www.fdncenter.org

Mission is to foster public understanding of the foundation field. Grantmaker services include: foundation folders, electronic grant reporting and grants classification. The center collects, organizes, analyzes and disseminates information on foundations.

Indiana University - Center on Philanthropy
550 West North Street, Suite 301
Indianapolis, IN 46202-3272
Phone:317 274-4200 Fax: 317 684-8900
Website: www.philanthropyiupui.edu

A national resource for education, research, training and public service programs in the not-for-profit sector. Philanthropic studies library, archives, degree programs and executive leadership programs available.

National Center for Family Philanthropy
1220 Nineteenth Street NW, Suite 804
Washington, DC 20036
Phone: 202 293-3424   Fax: 202 293-3395
Website: www.ncfp.org

Founded to encourage individuals and families to create and sustain a
philanthropic mission. Provides resource materials, publishes a journal
and monographs; sponsors educational programs; has two documents
to assist those beginning foundations; their journal articles include
investment issues, donor legacy, and the value of a family's philanthropy across generations.

The Philanthropy Roundtable
1150 17th Street NW, Suite 503
Washington, DC 20036
Phone: 202 822-8333   Fax: 202 822-8325
E-mail: main@philanthropyroundtable.org
Website: www.philanthropyroundtable.org

A national association of individual donors, foundation staff and
trustees, corporate giving representatives, trust and estate officers.
Considers voluntary private action via the private sector as critical to
creating wealth that makes philanthropy possible.